WORLD FAMOUS
ROYAL SCANDALS

WORLD FAMOUS
ROYAL
SCANDALS

Rowan Wilson

This edition published and distributed by Parragon,
produced by Magpie Books,
and imprint of Robinson Publishing, London

Parragon
Unit 13–17,
Avonbridge Trading Estate,
Atlantic Road,
Avonmouth,
Bristol, BS11 9QD

ISBN 0 75251 784 8

British Library Cataloguing-in-Publication Data
A catalogue record for this book is available
from the British Library

10 9 8 7 6 5 4 3 2 1

CONTENTS

Chapter one: **The Fat Philanderer**   1

Chapter two: **Queen Caroline – The only British Queen to be tried for Adultery**   23

Chapter three: **The King who wanted to be a Commoner**   29

Chapter four: **Chaos and Scandal in Serbia**   47
(1) The Gypsy King   47
(2) The King and the Commoner   57

Chapter five: **The Mayerling Affair**   81

Chapter six: **Queen Victoria and John Brown**   89

Chapter seven: **Ludwig and Lola**   103

Chapter eight: **The King and Mrs Simpson**   119

Chapter nine: **The Buckingham Palace Security Scandal**   141

Chapter ten: **Annus Horribilis**   147
Prince Charles, Lady Diana and Other Royal Scandals   147

Chapter One

THE FAT
PHILANDERER

In the last days of October, 1788, King George III began
to lose his reason. The signs were familiar to those
around him, for he had hovered on the brink of madness on
a number of occasions. These episodes had, of course, been
carefully hidden from the British public.

The symptoms that began appear that October were
more disturbing than in the earlier attacks. It started with
back pains and convulsions, then the king began to suffer
from hallucinations. A page saw him holding a conversation with an oak tree, apparently under the delusion that it
was the King of Prussia. After that, the king's urine turned
brown, his eyes became bloodshot, and he began to foam
at the mouth. The royal household did its best to remain
calm and stoical, but there was an increasing sense of
panic.

The problem, quite simply, was who would succeed him.
For Prince George, the heir to the throne, was one of the
most habitual drunks and profligate spendthrifts in the
country. This is why the Prime Minister, William Pitt the
Younger, gave orders that the strictest secrecy was to be
observed about the king's illness. (It did no good, of course;
the rumours were soon all over the country.) Pitt had more
reason than than anyone to dread the idea of the prince
becoming George IV, for the prince had been one of his
major headaches for the past year or so.

To understand why, it is necessary to say something
about the prince's earlier life.

When, in 1762, King George III's first born proved to be a son, there had been rejoicing throughout the land. King George was a level-headed and modest man, obsessed by the notions of royal duty and clean, healthy family life, and he would eventually father fifteen children.

Everyone hoped that his son, Prince George, would in due course make as good a king as his amiable father. Unfortunately, as the young man matured, this began to look increasingly doubtful. Even as a child the prince displayed a taste for flattery and a fondness for over-eating, flaws that were encouraged by his uncles, whom the boy admired rather more than he did his father. For the king's austere morality was not shared by his siblings. The Dukes of Gloucester and Cumberland in particular were notorious drunks and womanisers, who enjoyed disgracing the House of Hanover in drinking establishments and gambling clubs all over London. Young George greatly preferred them to his incredibly dull father.

The prince's education was partly to blame. He had been taught all about the liberal arts, and the skills of a sportsman, but nothing about history or economics, the kind of thing that might have been useful to a good ruler. As it was his main ambition seemed to be to develop into a world-class seducer and alcoholic.

History fails to record his first steps down the primrose path. Some say that it began with his seduction of one of his mother's maids of honour, others that his first conquest was the Duchess of Cumberland, his uncle's wife — originally a widow named Mrs Anne Horton — who enlivened any gathering to which she was invited by telling risque jokes in a voice that carried all over the room. The former Mrs Horton was just the kind of person, who would enjoy introducing a young man to the facts of life. But whether she did or not, there can be no doubt that Prince George's sexual exploits began well before he was in his mid-teens. In fact, he was only sixteen when his father felt it necessary to send him a letter criticising his drinking and whoring. It was the first of many similar letters, and their tone suggests that King George himself deserves some of the blame; less irritation and more sympathetic understanding might have achieved better results.

> A memorandum from the Royal Archives, sent by the Prince Regent, later King George IV, to his brother William, later King William IV reads:
>   'Last night I fucked two whores – I hope I don't catch a dose.'

The prince was not his father's only headache. The king became so disgruntled about the exploits of his brothers, and rumours that they were all bigamously married to ladies like Mrs Horton, that in 1772 he introduced the Royal Marriage Act, under which marriage to Catholics and divorcees was illegal, and any royal marriage required the king's approval. This would lead indirectly to the greatest scandal of the prince's inglorious career.

At the same time as he was losing his son to wine and women, King George was losing America to its rebel colonists. His high-principled, moralistic attitudes, which created a sense of stability in times of peace, only aroused irritation in people with grievances, like the over-taxed Bostonians. For all his good intentions, the king seemed doomed to cause misunderstandings.

Prince George's first public affair began when he was eighteen. Seated in the royal box at Covent Garden, watching a performance of *The Winter's Tale*, George was dazzled by the beauty of the actress playing Perdita. Whenever she approached his side of the stage, the prince would lean out of the box and – to the amusement of the audience – gaze at her with forlorn adoration.

Her name was Mary Robinson, she was just 21, and George learned – from his chaperon Lord Malden – that she was married to a young clerk in a law office. Brushing aside this complication, George called for pen and ink, and wrote her a love letter, which he signed Florizel – the name of Perdita's lover in the play. The choice of pseudonym was also meant to imply that, like Perdita, Mary Robinson was a princess in disguise. To Lord Malden's horror, George demanded that his chaperon deliver the letter to Mrs Robinson backstage.

Mary Robinson read the letter, which she assumed came from Lord Malden, and told him wearily to go away. Her skills as an actress – combined with her scanty pastoral costumes – brought her flocks of admirers. When Lord Malden grasped the cause of the misunderstanding, and explained that the letter was from Prince George, he noted that the lady became perceptibly more interested . . .

But in spite of a series of charmingly-written love letters, Mary Robinson declined to meet Prince Florizel. She was flattered and not a little tempted – for George was a handsome young man, and his waistline was still under control – but she feared the reaction of the king. The prince's scandalous sexual adventures were already common knowledge, and so was his father's disapproval. And while the prince could not compel her into his bed, the king could certainly destroy her acting career, which was the only thing that stood between her and debtors' prison she had only recently escaped.

The lovelorn prince continued to attend the play every night, often staring so intensely that Mary forgot her lines. She was determined to remain faithful to her husband – at least, until one night when she returned home from a performance earlier than usual, and caught her husband in bed with the maid. At that point, she wrote George a

George, Prince of Wales

reply. She would meet him – but on one condition: that George's younger brother Frederick should be present. It was known that the king's brothers were more serious-minded than George. Mary Robinson trusted that Frederick would restrain the Crown Prince should he lose control of his libido.

The meeting had to be secret, in case the king found out, so it was arranged that Lord Malden should take Mary to dinner at a riverside inn near the royal palace. Then, well after dark, he would row her across the river, where George, having sneaked out with his younger brother, would be waiting.

All went according to plan, and the four of them met in the darkness. George was trembling with tension at the prospect of being closer than twenty feet to his beloved. But this rather crowded lovers' tryst ended abruptly when lights and shouting from the palace indicated that the king had heard some suspicious noises and had sent his equerries to investigate. Lord Malden and Mary quickly jumped back into the boat and rowed away. The princes had to hide in the bushes until the furore died down . . .

Mary's nerves had been shaken by these alarums and excursions, and ignored George's pleas for another meeting – she was aware that if the king caught them together, her career was finished. Recognizing that his tender pleas were a waste of time, George decided to offer a more substantial inducement. In his next letter, among the passionate protestations of undying love, he offered her twenty thousand pounds if she would become his mistress. This, the practical Mary thought, was a bit more like it. She agreed immediately, explaining her change of heart by declaring that she had finally succumbed to 'the irresistable sweetness of his smile, the tenderness of his melodious yet manly voice'. But before fulfilling her part of the bargain, she made sure that George signed an undertaking to pay her the £20,000 as soon as he came of age – until then he had to make do with a small allowance. So Mary Robinson settled in a house whose rent was paid by the prince, and George finally had his way with her.

There was no hint of intrigue about the affair. Everyone knew about it from the start. Cartoons portraying Perdita and Florizel drawn to look like the pair were displayed in London shop-windows. Anyone who had missed the message could not fail to remark that Mrs Robinson, previously only moderately well-off, now rode around London in a four-horse carriage with two servants perched on the back. Moreover, she wore a picture of George around her neck in public. She found that being a royal mistress was more fun than she had expected.

George, on the other hand, was already regretting the bargain. He was too young to realise that, after so much anticipation, even a night with Cleopatra would have been an anticlimax, and – like all spoilt and selfish people – was inclined to put the blame on the lady. Within weeks he was tired of her, and transferred his attentions to a Mrs Grace Dalrymple, the divorced wife of a Harley Street doctor.

Trusting to the postal service to end the affair, just as it had begun it, George wrote Mrs Robinson a brief letter in which he explained that they could never meet again, since he had learned that she had insulted one of his friends in public. (This was, of course, an excuse he had invented.) But Mary had no intention of being abandoned. She persuaded George to meet her, and found him so pleasant that she imagined they were back on their old footing again. The next day, she came upon the prince in Hyde Park, and was shocked and upset when he looked straight past her.

Their correspondence continued, but it had now deteriorated into accusations and counter-accusations. And when she realised that there was no chance of getting him back, Mary finally did what she had been hoping to avoid – hinted to Lord Malden that she would make use of the document promising her £20,000, and the prince's love

7

letters, which made it clear why he felt she was worth so much.

This hint of public exposure sobered the prince. The problem was that he had no way of laying his hands on such a vast sum — more than half a million in modern money. Lord Malden was authorised by George to offer five thousand pounds. Mrs Robinson scoffed at the offer. Her debts, she said, amounted to six hundred pounds more than that.

In the end George had to give in. The five thousand was accepted, accompanied by a pension of five hundred pounds a year for life. On Mrs Robinson's death, her daughter would continue to receive half that amount for life. The letters would be returned, along with a letter from George agreeing that the papers had not been sold, but given freely.

Now the problem was to raise the £5,000. George was forced to tell his father the whole story. The king was furious, and the prince had to sit through a tantrum that lasted most of the morning. And then, since the king did not have the money either, he had to go to his Prime Minister, and beg him to try and raise it. Lord North solved the problem by quietly adding the figure to that year's Secret Service budget — in effect, embezzling the tax payer. The king dug in his heels about Mrs Robinson's pension, declaring that his son could find that out of his own allowance.

So Mary received her pay-off, and the first instalment on her pension, and went off to live in Paris. Many years later she would return to England, become the mistress of a member of Parliament, and renew her friendship with the prince. When she died — twenty years after the affair — her daughter continued to receive £250 a year.

This episode finally convinced King George that his son was totally irresponsible. So while his brothers were given commissions in the army, George was left with no royal duties and, moreover, was kept surrounded by a cordon of equerries to keep him out of mischief. In response, the prince began drinking more heavily than ever, and showed his disgust by ignoring the equerries. Since they could not physically restrain him, George spent his evenings drinking and whoring around London with disreputable members of the peerage. His love affairs were conducted openly, and he ran up enormous debts that he had no hope of paying.

What worried the king rather more was that the prince had taken a great liking to two members of the Whig opposition Charles James Fox and Richard Brinsley Sheridan. Like the prince, Fox was a keen gambler who was known to spend most of the day and night at the card table, from which he would rush off to attend the House, then return to gamble for the rest of the night. Sheridan was, of course, an immensely popular playwright – a disreputable profession in itself.

Fox and Sheridan clearly had practical motives for cultivating the prince's friendship. In effect, they were staking their claim – for one day George would be king, and then the time would come for the repayment of debts. This is what worried the king.

By the time George turned 21, in 1783, he had a great many debts, and asked his father for money to support an independent establishment. Fox, who was then Foreign Secretary, did his best to pull strings in Parliament, but ran into opposition from the king. Finally, Parliament was persuaded to settle George's present debts – £30,000 – and allow him another £30,000 to move into Carlton House, in Pall Mall. The prince repaid Fox's support by voting for his India Bill, which failed. But Carlton House turned into an anti-Tory stronghold.

George was already involved in his maddest love affair so far. The lady was a beautiful widow named Maria Fitzherbert. She was 28, six years George's senior, and had been twice married. George fell instantly and violently in love with her when he saw her sitting in friend's box at the opera, and pursued her with his usual single mind-edness. But Mrs Fitzherbert was more a difficult catch than Mary and others like her. To begin with, she had private means, so could not be bought. Second, she was a devout Catholic, and was aware that the Royal Marriage Act was directed against Catholics; it was not that – at that time – she had any wish to marry the prince, but she felt that such discrimination was unfair.

George pursued her with the same wild passion he had shown for Mary Robinson. She was flattered, found him likeable, but had no intention of becoming his mistress. George found it incomprehensible that anyone could refuse to give him his own way. He flew into tantrums and burst into tears, and talked endlessly to anyone who would listen about Mrs Fitzherbert. (Part of his charm was that he did not stand on his dignity, unless he was in a bad mood.) But Mrs Fitzherbert had heard all about Mary Robinson and her numerous successors, and had no intention of being wooed and then deserted. Finally, she decided it would be simplest if she left England.

When he heard about it, George collapsed on his couch in an agony of grief. No previous conquest had ever been this difficult. The prospect of losing something he wanted so much made him feel he was going mad. In a grand romantic gesture George attempted suicide by falling on his sword. 'Attempt' was the key word, since he all but missed. He was found, bloody but only superficially wounded, lying on his couch.

Four royal equerries went to Mrs Fitzberbert's house and finally prevailed on her to see him. She was reluctant, but agreed on condition she could take some lady of unassail-able reputation with her. The Duchess of Devonshire was persuaded to go, and the found the prince lying on the settee, his chest covered in blood. Rumour would later declare that his physician had bled him to relieve hysteria, and that he had simply torn off the bandages. But if it was a trick, it worked. When George showed her his wound, she was shaken, and began to feel that his threats of suicide were serious after all. George declared that he would make another attempt unless Mrs Fitzherbert agreed to marry him, and accepted a symbolic ring. Mrs Fitzherbert allowed herself to be convinced; she borrowed a ring from the Duchess of Devonshire, and placed it solemnly on her finger.

Back at home, Mrs Fitzherbert decided that it had all been a charade. The next day she left England, leaving no address.

George flew into another hysterical frenzy. Then he decided to pursue her to Europe. The king, he reasoned, would be glad to get rid of him — he had already spent far more than the £30,000 on Carlton House. But the king mistrusted the mild and casual way his son raised the matter, and decided it would be safer to refuse — after all, George could run up enormous debts abroad as easily as at home. And when he heard the gossip about the 'marriage' to Mrs Fitzherbert, he was relieved that he had no allowed himself to taken in. After the king's final refusal, George had another shrieking tantrum.

He had finally obtained Mrs Fitzherbert's address, and now kept up a stream of love letters. He was not used to this kind of frustration. He sobbed, beat his head on the wall, tore his hair. And when friends who wanted to see him reconciled with his father suggested that he ought to take a wife, George swore that he would never marry. He would emigrate to America with Mrs Fitzherbert . . .

After sixteen months of separation from his beloved, George wrote to her proposing marriage. She knew the idea was insane — that it would be illegal, and that no priest would dare to marry them. But George's devotion had finally convinced her that she loved him, and in late November, 1785, she returned to London. A few weeks

Maria Fitzherbert

12

later, she and George were married at a secret ceremony by a priest who had been released from Newgate debtors' prison. They then went off for a honeymoon at Richmond.

The marriage was soon the gossip of the London drawing rooms. But although the couple were often seen at the same social gatherings, even sitting at the same table, their relationship seemed to be one of friendly politeness. George's friends noted that he seemed more contented than he had ever been. Mrs Fitzherbert moved to a house in St James's Square, which was closer to Carlton House.

Unfortunately, George's new found happiness did not curtail his extravagance. By the end of 1785, he owed more than a quarter of a million pounds. He tried a subtle form a blackmail on the king, suggesting that he should close up Carlton House and dismiss the staff. The king recognized this for what it was – an attempt to force his hand by making him look mean, and ignored it. Fox managed to improve the situation by suggesting that most of the prince's allowance should be handled by trustees.

The prince decided that his relations with his father might improve if he moved further from London. Besides, he wanted an opportunity to live with his wife. Brighton had recently become a fashionable seaside resort, where the wealthy went to cure their ills by bathing in the sea. George moved there in 1786, bought a farmhouse on the sea front, and moved Mrs Fitzherbert in with him.

The months that followed were probably the happiest of his life. Yet although he was spending less money, his father showed no sign of wanting to persuade Parliament to pay off his debts. Something had to be done. George persuaded an independent Member of Parliament to raise the question in the House. The response of the Tory spokesman was that this was a delicate subject, because it involved matters concerning the Church and Constitution – a clear hint at the marriage with Mrs Fitzherbert. The loyal Sheridan rose to ask what they were hinting at. Mr Pitt, the Prime Minister, replied that if this matter of the prince's finances was pursued, he might be obliged to reveal something he would prefer to conceal. Sheridan replied that in that case, he should explain what he meant. Mr Pitt realised that he was treading on the edge of an abyss, and replied lamely that he was merely referring to the prince's debts.

> Catherine De Medici, Queen Regent of France in the 16th century, used a ceiling spyhole to watch her husband making love to his mistress.

George could see that trouble was looming. Next time Pitt might rise to the challenge, and then he would be faced with the problem of whether to deny the marriage or come clean. This time he turned to Fox for help. And when the marriage was again hinted at in the House, Fox rose to his feet and declared that the tales of the prince's marriage were a malicious falsehood. Fox, of course, knew this to be untrue, and he knew that he could be impeached for lying to Parliament, but he swallowed his misgivings, and perjured himself for his friend; after all, there was no harm in increasing the prince's debt of gratitude.

Typically, the prince was not in the least grateful. He actually wanted to tell Mrs Fitzherbert that it might be necessary to deny their marriage in public, but was too much of a coward to do it. And when Fox saved him the trouble, he rushed to Mrs Fitzherbert and told her indignantly that Fox had lied to Parliament. Far from understanding the problem, Mrs Fitzherbert was furious, and declined to see George. The prince had more bouts of fever and hysteria, for which he had to be bled. Finally, she forgave him, and they went off once more to Brighton, where George began to lose some of the weight he had been accumulating — at one point he weighed 16 stone — and tried hard to spend less money.

And it was at this point that the bombshell exploded. The king began to show unmistakable signs of insanity, and Parliament realised that this probably meant that Prince George would become king — or at least regent, the temporary guardian of the throne. The thought appalled everybody. If this drunken, womanising spendthrift came to the throne, he would bankrupt the country, and probably cause a revolution.

Pitt had another reason for anxiety. If the prince became king, it would mean the fall of the Tory government. Fox, Sheridan and his gang would soon be running the country.

Fox thought so too. He rushed home from Italy, and announced his opinion that if the king was mad, it was much the same as if the king was dead. Of course, the king might recover — but meanwhile, Prince George ought to be appointed regent.

Pitt cunningly turned his own argument against him. If the prince was to become regent, it would need royal assent. And if the king was mad, he could not assent to anything. Pitt was determined to delay the evil day as long as possible. If the worst came to the worst, he decided, he could always return to the Bar — his profession before entering politics.

Prince George hurried to see his father, and was shocked by his ravings. In his misery, the king abandoned all pretence of even liking his son. During dinner, he leapt to his feet, dragged George out of his chair, and hurled him against the wall. The prince was not as upset as he might have been. At least his father's feelings were out in the open, and he could also drop the pretence of loving the irascible old man. His parties at Carlton House became bigger, noisier and more expensive, and he achieved a new level of bad taste by entertaining his guests with imitations of his father's ravings.

What no one realised at the time was that the king was suffering from an illness called porphyria, which involves a problem with the creation of haemoglobin, the oxygen-carrying red component of blood. As a result, there is a build-up of brownish pigment — one of haemoglobin's components — which shows up in urine as a brown discolouration. Other symptoms are extreme sensitivity of the skin, and mental confusion. In effect, the sufferer's own body is poisoning him to death.

By now, the equerries who attended King George were exhausted. He did not sleep for more than a few hours at a time, which meant that the equerries had to sit in the king's bedroom all night. If he woke and found himself unat-tended, the king was likely to escape from the palace and wander around the grounds. The sensitivity of his skin also meant that shaving irritated him badly. On one occasion, having been persuaded by long argument to sit still and be shaved, the king jumped up and ran off half way through the operation. For the rest of the day he wandered the palace with half a beard.

The doctors guessed — correctly — that the problem was some kind of poison in his system, and they tried to cure it by blistering the king's legs, hoping the 'evil humours' would run out through the sores. This only made the king hate his doctors.

Finally, someone realised that it was the king's brain, not his blood, that was the problem. A clergyman named Willis, who ran a successful asylum for the insane, was called to the palace. When the king tried to make him go away with irritable shouts, Willis shouted back: 'Be calm!' No one had ever shouted at the king in his life, and he screamed even louder. Willis continued to shout back until the exhausted king lowered his voice.

Willis had brought a strait-jacket with him, and made it quite clear that he would use it if the king misbehaved. The king promptly lost his temper, and Willis carried out his threat. George was tied up in the jacket, and then tied to the bed. After that, the king was trussed up so regularly that a special chair was designed with leg irons and a gag for his mouth – he liked to refer to it as his throne.

Willis also persuaded the king to play board games, and noticed that, no matter how nonsensical his conversation, George never lost his grasp on the game and was always a formidable opponent.

In his illness, the king's conversation tended more and more towards sex – particularly how much he used to enjoy sex with the queen. One afternoon in late December, Willis decided that the king was calm enough to benefit from a visit from his wife. A courtier named Greville reports that, while standing guard outside the door, he heard George weeping. The proud and highly moral king had lost all his self-control and tried to rape his wife.

Meanwhile, back at Windsor, Prince George had taken control of the court. As everyone had feared, increased responsibility had no effect upon him. He was drinking and spending more heavily than ever. It was also clear that he was beginning to enjoy power. Every day he pressed Fox to use his influence to get him declared regent, and Fox – naturally – thought this an excellent idea. The bulletins from Kew showed that the king, although not getting any worse, was certainly not improving. Clearly, the prince argued, his unofficial position should be ratified by Parliament.

Understandably, Pitt disagreed. He was hoping against hope that the king would recover. The prince cursed him, and talked about a *coup d'etat*; he even began holding regular secret meetings with the Whigs. His opponents mobilized pamphleteers and satirists, who portrayed him as a drunken brawler. And George, who financial problems had earned him a great deal of sympathy from the British public, soon became one of the most unpopular men in the country.

Pitt knew he could have to give way sooner or later, and fought a grim rearguard action. If the prince had to be declared regent, at least Parliament could curtail his powers – keep his hands out of the national treasury, and prevent him from making peers and awarding pensions. The whole country was split between the prince's supporters, and those who felt that he would be the worst disaster that could befall Great Britain.

During Christmas 1788, the Tories were gloomy, and Prince George and the Whigs full of high spirits. Pitt's delaying tactics could not last forever, and when he had to concede defeat, that would be the end of his political career. Finally, in February 1789, Pitt knew he could go on no longer. It was time for Parliament to vote whether the prince would become Prince Regent. And, to Pitt's inexpressible relief, he won. The House voted that Prince George did not have an automatic right to power because his father was ill, and that the queen would remain head of the royal household.

Within weeks, it had become clear that the bill had been unnecessary. The king's doctors reported that he was beginning to recover. The prince refused to believe it, suspecting that it was all a plot to keep him out of power. Finally, he and his brother Frederick – who was showing signs of following in his brother's unsteady footsteps – managed to set up an appointment to see the king. The old man looked frail and exhausted, but there could be no doubt that he was no longer mad.

In their disappointment, George and Frederick went to Brooks's Club, and told everyone that the king was as ill as ever. Word got back to the queen, who was enraged. Next time they tried to visit the king, they were refused admittance. At a concert given at Windsor, to celebrate the king's recovery, both princes were treated with frozen disapproval. Later, when a service of thanksgiving was given at St Paul's, the prince retaliated by munching biscuits and joking under his breath with his brother Frederick.

His brief taste of power had been tantalizing and George accepted its loss with a bad grace. His gambling and drinking provided cartoonists with endless material for satire – one cartoon showed him drunk with his head in his arms, his fat belly bursting out of his trousers, and surrounded by empty wine bottles, while in the background there are piles of unpaid bills and cures for venereal disease. Never had an heir to the British throne fallen into such low esteem.

George did nothing to improve his image. His debts now at £400,000, he had to borrow the money from Holland. He spent recklessly on a stable at Newmarket, then had to withdraw from racing when it was suggested that he had gambled on one of own horses in a fixed race. Over the years he grew bored with Mrs Fitzherbert, and she finally decided to break with him when, at a royal dinner, she was told she had no fixed place at table, and would have to sit according to her rank.

By that time, in an attempt to raise money for his creditors, George had allowed himself to be dragooned into marrying a princess named Caroline of Brunswick. When he saw her for the first time he was horrified; she was fat, coarse and personally unhygienic. At the marriage ceremony he was drunk. Even so, Parliament refused to pay his debts – now £600,000. England was at war with France and could not afford such a sum. After dutifully impregnating her, the prince found himself unable to remain in the same room with her, let alone continue to sleep with her, and within a year wrote her a letter explaining that 'our inclinations are not within our power', and made sure she moved elsewhere.

When the prince separated from Caroline, she made sure that the British public knew how badly she had been treated, and her husband's popularity declined to such an extent that he did not dare to show his face in London for fear of being attacked by the mob.

In 1810 the king's mind collapsed again, and George was finally sworn in as regent. He immediately enraged the Whigs by refusing to keep any of his promises.

In 1820 the Prince Regent finally became King George. To his embarrassment, Caroline reappeared and demand her rights as queen. The country supported her, and George's popularity reached a new low when she was locked out of Westminster Abbey at his coronation. Her death less than a month later resolved the situation, but as her body was taken through London to Germany, there were riots in the streets.

As King George, he was less bad than expected — largely because age had reduced his capacity for debauchery. He confined his extravagance to projects like modernizing Windsor Castle, building the British Museum and National Gallery, and planning the royal home that would become Buckingham Palace. An attempt to interfere in international politics was foiled by his Prime Minister George Canning, but he solaced himself with a new mistress, Lady Conyngham, and began spending much of his time in a 'cottage' in Windsor Park, which he preferred to the Castle. In the last six years of his reign, his excesses caught up with him, and he began to spend most of his time in bed with gout and bladder problems. His seven year old niece Victoria sat on his fat knee, and found him disgusting because his face was covered with greasepaint, which he wore to hide his wrinkles. As his weight increased, he found it increasingly difficult to walk, and became so paranoid about his appearance that he dismissed any servant he caught looking at him. His last political defeat came in 1829, when a bill to allow Catholics to sit in Parliament was passed in spite of his bitter opposition.

Finally, his weight led to attacks of breathlessness that caused his face and finger-ends to go black. Mrs Fitzherbert, in exile at Brighton (with a £6,000 a year pension) wrote him a tender letter, which he placed beneath his pillow. She still loved him; but the king did not dare to allow her to come and see what he had turned into; instead he increased her pension to £10,000. In June 1830, his strength began to fade, and on 26 June, to the relief of most of his subjects, he died at the age of 67.

Chapter Two

QUEEN CAROLINE – THE ONLY BRITISH QUEEN TO BE TRIED FOR ADULTERY

It is something of a mystery why the Prince of Wales, the son of King George III, agreed to marry the fat, ugly and tactless Caroline of Brunswick. It is true that he did it largely to persuade parliament to pay his enormous debts. But he could have married the queen's niece, the beautiful and talented Louise of Mecklenburg-Strelitz. His marriage to Caroline was a disaster for everyone.

George Augustus Frederick, the Prince of Wales, was born in August 1762. Determined that his son would grow up virtuous and serious-minded, George III had him brought up far from the court, according to a strict academic and physical regimen. It had the opposite effect: the prince became a rebel, a spendthrift and a waster. At the age of seventeen he embarked on an affair with an actress, Mary Robinson, and his letters to her had to be bought back eventually for £5,000. The prince became a member of a hard-drinking, hard-gambling set, which included the Whig politician Charles James Fox – one of his father's chief enemies – and the playwright Sheridan. He began to run up vast debts. He voted for Fox – and against his father – when Fox's India Bill came before parliament but the Whig politician lost and was dismissed. When he was twenty-three, the prince fell in love with the beautiful

Catholic, Mrs Fitzherbert, and although she fled to France
to escape his attentions, he finally persuaded her to go
through a secret marriage. But constancy was not one of his
strong points and he soon took another mistress, Lady
Jersey.

By the time he was thirty, the prince was an embarrassment to his father and intensely unpopular with the British
public. His debts now amounted to £630,000 – many
millions in present-day terms – and Pitt's administration
showed no eagerness to find the money. So when it was
suggested by his father that he should marry and furnish an
heir, he agreed on condition that parliament paid his debts.

Caroline of Brunswick was short, plump and ugly, and
she suffered from body odour – probably as a result of
infrequent washing. Lady Jersey, the prince's current mistress, may have pushed him into marrying Caroline rather
than the beautiful Louise of Mecklenburg-Strelitz as she
would be less of a rival. On 5 April 1795, at St James's
Palace, the prince was introduced to Caroline; he was
shattered. He staggered to the far end of the room and
called for a brandy. He went on drinking brandy for three
days until the marriage ceremony. On the honeymoon –
with Lady Jersey also in attendance – he seems to have
done his duty as a husband, for Caroline discovered she was
pregnant soon thereafter. But the prince found her unbear-
able and stayed as far away from her as possible; in the
following year he wrote her a letter saying that, 'our
inclinations are not in our power', but that being polite
to one another was. When she received the letter, Queen
Caroline was with the politician George Canning and asked
him what he thought it meant; Canning replied that it
seemed to give her permission to do as she liked. Whereupon Queen Caroline proceeded to do just that with
Canning.

What no one realized at the time was that the royal line
of Hanover suffered from the disease known as porphyria,

the 'royal disease', a genetic disorder in which, due to an enzyme defect, the body accumulates large quantities of porphyrins (precursors of red blood pigment). The disease affects the digestive tract, the nervous system, the circulatory system and the skin; it causes psychotic disorders and epilepsy. George III had several attacks of it and died insane. The Prince of Wales was also subject to it and so was Caroline — two of her brothers were imbeciles, probably due to porphyria. It may explain Caroline's utter lack of self-control and her tendency to behave outrageously which led many to suspect she was insane.

Rejected by her husband she retired to a house in Blackheath and behaved in a manner that led Lady Hester Stanhope to call her 'a downright whore'. She had a Chinese clockwork figure in her room which, when wound up, performed gross sexual movements; she was also given to dancing around in a manner that exposed a great deal of her person.

In 1806, rumours that a four year old child in her entourage, William Austin, was her illegitimate son, led to what became known as 'the Delicate Investigation'. A Royal Commission repudiated the charge and found Lady Douglas, who had started the rumour, guilty of perjury. But years later, Caroline told her lawyer's brother that the child was the natural son of Prince Louis Ferdinand of Prussia, who had always been her love. Mrs Fitzherbert was to state later that Caroline had secretly married Prince Louis before she married the Prince of Wales.

Finally, in August 1814, Caroline decided to leave England. In Geneva, at a ball given in her honour, she shocked her hosts by dancing naked to the waist. In Naples she became the mistress of King Joachim, Napoleon's brother-in-law. When she left Naples — at the time Napoleon escaped from Elba — she had with her Napoleon's courier, a coarsely handsome Italian named Bartolomeo Bergami, a former quartermaster in a regiment of hussars.

Royal Scandals

This swarthy, bearded, intensely masculine character looked like a brigand from a Drury Lane play. He travelled with her to Munich, Tunis, Athens, Constantinople and Jerusalem, and when they settled in her villa near Pesaro they behaved as man and wife.

James Brougham, her lawyer's brother, now wrote to England suggesting that the prince — he was now Prince Regent (his father having become insane) — should obtain a legal separation from Caroline so she could never become queen of England. But the prince wanted divorce or nothing. So nothing came of this suggestion.

George III finally died in January 1820 and his son became George IV. Caroline of Brunswick was now Queen Caroline. The government quickly offered her £50,000 a year if she would agree not to return to England. In a fury, Caroline hurried across the Channel. Her husband was one of the most unpopular men in the country and on that count many people espoused her cause. To the intense embarrassment of the government, she settled at Brandenburg House, in Hammersmith. And on 17 August the government took the offensive by hauling her in front of the House of Lords. Its aim was to dissolve the marriage on the grounds that Caroline had engaged in 'a most unbecoming and degrading intimacy' with Bergami, 'a foreigner of low station'. But the government had bitten off more than it could chew. Noisy mobs demonstrated in favour of Caroline and the House of Lords had to be surrounded by two strong timber fences. The queen's coach was always surrounded by a cheering crowd. After fifty-two days the divorce clause was carried. But the oratory of Henry Brougham caused a turn in the tide and when the Bill was given its final reading, it had only a pathetic majority of nine. The Lords decided to drop it.

The coronation was scheduled for 29 April 1821. The queen wrote to the Prime Minister, Lord Liverpool, to ask what kind of a dress she ought to wear for the coronation. He replied that she could 'form no part of that ceremony'. But when George was crowned, Caroline arrived at the Abbey dressed in a muslin slip and demanded to be admitted. When she shouted, 'The queen – open!', pages opened the doors. She continued with 'I am the queen of England.' An official roared, 'Do your duty, shut the Hall door,' and the door was slammed in her face. Undaunted, Caroline drove back to Brandenburg House and sent a note to the king asking for a coronation 'next Monday'.

She died two weeks later, on 7 August 1821 – so suddenly that it was widely rumoured that she had been poisoned. When her body was on its way to the ship that would take it back to Brunswick, there were riots at Kensington Church, bricks were thrown, and two men were shot by the Life Guards. Caroline was buried in Brunswick Cathedral, with an inscription on her coffin: The Injured Queen Of England.

George IV remained intensely unpopular. He lived on for only nine years after the death of Caroline. The major issue of the time was Roman Catholic emancipation (England had been anti-Catholic since the time of Elizabeth I, and George I had come to the throne of England from Hanover because of the Act that prevented a Catholic from becoming king of England.) As Prince of Wales, George had been in favour of Wellington who, as prime minister, carried the act of parliament that finally achieved Catholic emancipation (although Wellington was himself basically opposed to it, believing it would finally destroy English rule in Ireland – as it did). George IV became hysterical about the issue and threatened to use the royal veto. But the throne no longer held the political power it had under George III, and he was reluctantly forced to accept Catholic emancipation. After that, the king's health deteriorated swiftly and he died on 26 June 1830. He had a portrait of Mrs Fitzherbert round his neck on his death bed. But the two had been estranged for many years — ever since, at a dinner in honour of Louis XVIII in 1803, he had made sure there was no fixed place for her at table, so she must sit 'according to her rank'. After that insult, she had retired from the court.

Chapter Three

THE KING WHO WANTED TO BE A COMMONER

When, on 29 January 1749, a son was born to the Royal house of Denmark, the court breathed a sigh of relief. Although King Frederick V, (known to his people as Frederick the Good) was only twenty-five, he seemed likely to die without an heir due to his prodigious alcoholism. In fact, when his son Christian came into the world, Frederick the Good was already more than halfway through his short life.

Christian's mother Queen Louise, a daughter of George II, died when the young prince was only three. Frederick soon remarried; his wife was Princess Juliana-Maria of Brunswick Wolfen-buettel. The new queen made no secret of her dislike of her stepson — after all, he would stand between her own children and the throne — and this increased when her first child was born weak and sickly. So from the time he could walk, the future king Christian had to endure a mother who loathed him and a father who lavished affection and kindness upon him only when he was sober enough to recognize him.

The nobleman appointed as his tutor, Count Reventlow, belonged to the old fashioned school who believed that sparing the rod would spoil even the most timid and browbeaten child, and would often beat him until the boy foamed at the mouth. (From the descriptions given by courtiers it seems likely that Christian was mildly epileptic.) Lack of emotional security and fear of being flogged turned the prince into a solitary, introverted child, mistrustful of kindness and inclined to daydream. His only friend was the page who served him, a boy named Sperling — a born rogue, who regarded his betters as his natural prey, and who taught Christian how to lie convincingly and devise pranks to spite the grown ups. Some courtiers have suggested in their memoirs that consorting with a commoner was the source of all Christian's later problems, and they could just be right.

As a result of Sperling's lessons in hypocrisy and deceit, Christian soon learned how to look and sound as smooth as the most two-faced courtier. But he shared Sperling's contempt for the upper classes; it seemed to him that commoners had far more fun than kings. So from an early age he daydreamed about becoming 'ordinary', as working class boys daydream about running away to sea.

He also had a more curious ambition. A tutor named Reverdil — who, unlike Count Reventlow, was friendly and well-meaning — records an occasion when he was unable, no matter how he tried, to gain the prince's attention. The boy ignored him, and went on poking himself in the chest and examining his legs. Many years later, Christian explained how, at the age of five, he had seen a troupe of Italian actors perform at court, and was spellbound. To his childish eyes, actors were far more impressive than mere kings and queens; they were gods, invulnerable and all powerful. Ever since that time he had daydreamed about becoming one of these deities, and kept abreast of his progress by poking himself hard to see if it hurt, and examining his legs to see whether they were as shapely as those of the leading man.

Reverdil also describes how the prince came to develop another of his obsessions — the neurotic fear that he was about to be dragged off to prison. One day, to alleviate the gloomy austerity of the child's life, one of the king's advisers suggested a special entertainment – a kind of royal variety show. Reventlow naturally disapproved, but finally agreed on condition that Christian should not be told beforehand – otherwise he might be distracted from his school work. The day arrived; the prince was to be taken to the entertainment in a carriage at the end of his morning lessons. As usual, Reventlow beat and bellowed at him until the very last moment. Then Christian was led away, his behind still smarting, to the waiting carriage. Since nobody had bothered to tell him what was happening, the bewildered prince was convinced he was being taken to prison, past rows of soldiers beating drums and saluting. In this state of terror, the entertainment seemed to be a kind of disconnected and surreal prelude to his imprisonment. Years later, when he was king, Christian admitted that he was unable to think of the occasion without breaking into a cold sweat of panic and helplessness.

Although brutal, Reventlow's teaching methods proved effective, and Christian performed brilliantly in his exams which were oral and held in public. He recited the answers to rehearsed questions for over three hours, delighting the gathered courtiers, who were convinced that, unlike the present drunken ignoramus, their future king would be a man of wit and learning. But the kindly Reverdil showed greater insight when he expressed doubts about the prince's education – no economics or statecraft, none of the essential knowledge required by a king – as just absurd bits of useless learning.

By now Frederick the Good was permanently drunk, and his health was seriously impaired. When, in 1757, he contracted pleurisy, his ministers consulted physicians about a fictitious patient with the king's symptoms. Unanimously, they all declared that unless the patient gave up his debauched lifestyle, he would be dead within the year. Told of this, Frederick became tearful and cursed his insatiable appetite for alcohol – then did his best to drown his sorrows by drinking twice as much. He spent most of his last year in bed, giving incomprehensible orders, such as that his army should be put on the Prussian Footing, when everyone knew perfectly well that he did not know what the Prussian Footing was.

Christian was deeply shaken by his father's illness — not just because the king had shown him affection during his sober periods, but because it meant that he now had to brace himself for the position he had always dreaded. So on the morning of 14 January, 1766, as Count Holcke announced to the hushed crowd: 'King Frederick is dead. Long live King Christian VII,' Christian looked as pale and dejected as if it was his own death that was being announced. He had been looking forward to the time when his education was finished, and he could enjoy being Crown Prince, travelling around Europe, seducing chambermaids and playing cards. Now these hopes had evaporated.

So, in 1766, at the age of 17, Prince Christian became King Christian VII of Denmark. It would be pleasant to record that the first thing he did was to have Count Reventlow hanged, or at least flogged. In fact, he allowed him to remain Court Chamberlain. But as he became more accustomed to authority, the king also took to contradicting his Chamberlain, and on one occasion disagreed with him so irritably that Reventlow came near to collapse; the king, suddenly frightened, rushed to get water to revive him. After that, Reventlow threatened to resign, and the king had to beg him to stay. But now he was aware that he was the master, and he took care that his former tormentor did not forget it.

A king, of course, needed a queen. Only a year earlier, Frederick the Good had planned a marriage for the Crown Prince. A likely bride had been located in England: Princess Carolina-Mathilda, daughter of the Prince of Wales and a sister of George III. The prospective bride was a pretty girl of fifteen, and when her portrait was received in Copenhagen, Christian had stared at it with obvious pleasure, and placed it on his writing desk. But now he was king, he seemed in no hurry to get married. He probably felt that he was being denied the opportunity — which every young nobleman should have — of sowing his wild oats.

In fact, as soon as he was king he tried to make up for lost time, and began casting his eye over some of the prettier ladies-in-waiting and their chambermaids. Christian had good looks and charm, and his position naturally made him twice as attractive; a number of girls seemed to like the idea of becoming the royal mistress. Christian's ministers recognized the symptoms — Frederick the Good had also had a roving eye. So they lost no time in sending for Carolina-Matilda.

She proved to be as pretty as her portrait, with a white skin and well-developed figure, and Christian seemed to lose his objections to allowing her to share his bed. He even began to display a certain exuberance. As he was dancing with her in the palace at Fredericksburg, he suddenly told one of the princes — who was dancing with his wife — to lead the dance through the rooms of the palace. When they arrived at the door of Carolina-Matilda's apartments, they found their way barred by an indignant lady-in-waiting, the highly respectable Madame de Plessen. The king exclaimed: 'Ignore the old woman,' and the dance proceeded through the queen's chambers and out the other side, to the fury of Madame de Plessen. From that point on, the king marked her down as one of those who would have to go.

The marriage was celebrated, and at first the king seemed well satisfied with his pretty bride. Then he began to grow restive. In the 18th century, it was unfashionable to be in love with one's wife, when every king had half a dozen mistresses. In any case, Christian enjoyed spending a night on the town with boon companions, and Copenhagen was full of serving wenches who felt that the handsome young king was their rightful lord and master.

Royal Scandals

So, accompanied by his former page Sperling, Christian set out to bed every attractive woman in Denmark, whether married or unmarried. It soon became clear that his appetite for drink easily matched that of his father. Yet his tedium threshold also seemed to be disquietingly low, and extravagant masques, balls and theatrical performances funded by the Royal purse were held every few days. Even so, Christian moved the court from castle to castle whenever a hangover convinced him that life was losing its sparkle. He seemed puzzled by the fact that a king, who could do anything he liked, should find it so hard to make his life entertaining.

Most of the court rather enjoyed the new regime; while a minority looked forward to the day when the king would eventually tire of extravagance and self-indulgence, and show some interest in the serious business of levying taxes and running the state, the rest decided that they might as well enjoy the party while it lasted.

When it finally became obvious that Christian was going to carry on amusing himself until the coffers were empty, his officials began to worry. Two years after his accession, Christian seemed to be getting more eccentric than ever. There were strange rumours regarding his pages – apparently he regularly ordered them to flog him, ,and those who beat the hardest received the most handsome presents. Christian also enjoyed pretending that he was being broken on the wheel. While Sperling, dressed as an executioner, would stand beside him with a scroll that was supposed to be a Death Warrant, the king would howl pathetically and gnash his teeth. Reventlow's chickens were coming home to roost.

Worse still, Christian had started a relationship with 'Milady', the most famous prostitute in Copenhagen. The pair indulged in bouts of drunken violence, and roamed the streets in the early hours of the morning smashing windows and street-lamps. On these occasions, the king would dress

The King who wanted to be a Commoner

John Frederick Struensee

as a commoner, convinced that no one would recognize him. On one occasion he even led an attack on the premises of some rival courtesans who, Milady declared, had insulted her. They broke down the doors of the house, smashed the windows and threw the furniture out into the street.

The people of Copenhagen had at first looked with indulgence on these pranks; they felt it made the king seem more human. But as they repaired their broken shopfronts and trampled gardens, their patience began to wear thin. On several occasions irritable citizens responded to his drunken insults by beating him up. And one evening, when he was recognized making his way back from Milady's house in plain clothes, he was pursued to the doors of the palace by an angry crowd who shouted insults.

Ministers might find it impossible to act against the king, but they could act against Milady. Afer she had persuaded the king to give her a mansion and the title of baroness, a group of determined court officials waited on the king, and refused to leave until he had signed an order of banishment. Milady was sent to Hamburg and kept confined.

What could be done? The king was the king. No one had a right to forbid him to do anything he chose to do. If he had been brought up to love and respect his advisers, all might have been different. But he had only learned to fear and detest them.

There was one obvious solution: persuade him to take a long holiday abroad. The king loved travel, and ever since a trip to Holstein in the previous year, was always badgering his ministers to arrange excursions. And, with a little luck, he might learn better manners in foreign courts . . .

So, on 6 May, 1768, Christian and his entourage, set out on a tour that would include Holland, Great Britain, France and Germany. The party numbered fifty-six, and included the king's newly appointed 'personal physician' John Frederick Struensee, whose secret brief was to act as

minder and bodyguard. It was – as we shall see – a
position that carried considerable power . . .

The queen was not one of the party; she had begged to
be allowed to go, but her husband had no intention of
allowing her to cramp his style. He was looking forward to
studying the lovemaking techniques of the women of the
rest of Europe.

Travelling under the name Count Travendahl, he began
by paying a visit to his brother-in-law Charles of Hesse,
husband of his favourite sister Louise, then travelled down
the Rhine to Cologne, then on to Amsterdam, then Brussels
and Calais. He found that he enjoyed travel so much that –
for the time being – he lost interest in prostitutes and
alcohol, and his entourage noted that his behaviour was
improving.

In Calais, he was met by the royal yacht *Mary*, sent by
his brother-in-law King George III, and they sailed for
Dover, where he resumed his rightful identity. But he began
to show signs of the old restiveness on being told that the
Archbishop of Canterbury intended to receive him with full
pomp and ceremony, and remarked irritably that the last
Danish king who had entered Canterbury had burned it to
the ground. It was plain to Struensee that the charm of
travel was beginning to wear off, and the king's attention
span, which had never been great, was being sorely tested
by official receptions.

It was the same when he met George III, and was
cornered by his mother-in-law, Dowager Princess Augusta
of Wales, who was worried about her daughter. As he
escaped from her interrogation he was heard to mutter in
French: 'That dear mama bores me sick.'

The man for whose ear this was intended was Count
Holck, a man whose chief achievements are described by
one historian as 'lying and dancing', and who was gradually
supplanting Sperling as the king's favourite accomplice in
mischief. While Struensee did his best to keep the king out

of trouble, Holck tried to establish himself in the royal favour by dangling temptations in front of his weak-willed sovereign. Struensee found it hard to compete.

Although regarded with disapproval by the staid and domesticated George III, Christian was loved by the common folk of London for his good looks and his readiness to join in their amusements. On one occasion, while dismounting from his coach outside St James' Palace, he was grabbed by a bosomy admirer, who shouted that even if she was killed for it, she would have a kiss from 'the prettiest fellow in the world'. Christian allowed her to embrace him, but decided to increase his bodyguard in case others tried to follow suit.

In London, the king soon settled down to leading the same life as in Copenhagen; he spent most of his time in taverns, and pursuing every woman who took his fancy. The pursuit was usually brief, since the poor in 18th century London lived at subsistence level, and no working class girl would afford to turn down a shilling as the price of her virtue, still less a purse full of guineas.

But what he enjoyed most was to play the part of Haroun Al Raschid and walk the streets of the capital incognito. This led to some amusing adventures. In a tavern in St Giles, he was paying court to a pretty girl who sold cherries when her lover – a huge Irishman – gave the king a light blow and told him to take his hand off her breast. The king slapped him back, and told him that he was ready to give satisfaction – to fight a duel. Count Holck intervened, and told the Irishman to let his brother alone. The Irishman replied that his brother had courage, and he liked him. 'Here is my hand.' The four of them consumed several glasses of gin, and the king was allowed to kiss the girl – in return for which he slipped his purse of guineas into her bosom.

He showed the same tolerance towards a City merchant with whom he had opened an account under the name of

The King who wanted to be a Commoner

Mr Frederickson. After the king had withdrawn £4,000, the merchant was so curious about his identity that he sent his boy to follow him. The boy duly reported that Mr Frederickson had entered St James's Palace by a private door, and that a sentry had told him that the gentleman must be a member of the king's suite. The next time Mr Frederickson called, the merchant and his wife invited him to drink tea, and while the wife was talking to Count Holck, the merchant took the king aside and asked him if the money was for King Christian. The king thought the merchant had guessed his identity, and when he realised this was not so, acknowledged that his host was correct.

'What is your post?', asked the merchant and Christian replied that it was mostly dressing the king and keeping him amused.

'I've heard he's a regular young profligate who spends money like water. I hope you make sure that you get your cut?'

The king assured him that he had never made a profit.

'What does the king do with so much money?'

'He gives it away to women – mostly in the form of jewels.'

'Good, then I've got a proposition for you. Why not let me buy the jewels . . .'

At that moment they were interrupted by a page, who asked if the King of Denmark was there.

The merchant shook his head. 'No, only a Mr Frederickson.'

'That *is* the king', said the page, 'He's the son of King Frederick.'

The merchant was so abashed that he hurried out of the room. Seeing that the lady was speechless, the king smiled reassuringly, and placed one of his rings on her finger. 'Please tell your husband that the king would never be offended by something that was said to Mr Frederickson in confidence.'

Christian's generosity was legendary. One one occasion, when he saw a tradesman being led to a debtor's prison, followed by his sobbing wife and children, he ordered his chamberlain to follow the coach and pay off the man's debts, as well as presenting him with £500. But most of his acts of generosity were less well-selected, and he often ended by flinging money away like confetti.

After eight weeks in London, Christian returned to the continent — to the relief of George III, who had come to dislike him intensely. The young officer named Gambier, who commanded the warship *Victoria* on which Christian sailed, would, almost forty years later, defeat the Danish fleet and bombard Copenhagen when the Danes sided with Napoleon.

Christian's next stop was Paris, which he found far more enjoyable than London. The French had no objection to a king who thought that amusement was the chief business of life, since most French kings subscribed to that opinion, and in this atmosphere of approval, Christian showed himself at his best, paying charming compliments and remaining wide awake at banquets. Painters painted his portrait, poets wrote verses to him, scholars addressed him in Latin, theatres staged special performances, and philosophers gathered around him and listened with flattering attention as he discoursed in perfect French. He also continued his studies in the amatory techniques of European womanhood by picking up prostitutes, barmaids and any passing beauty who took his fancy.

But it was in Paris that Count Holck noticed that the king's mind was wandering more than usual. He often lost track of a conversation, or stared blankly around him, as if he had plunged back into the daydreams in which he had spent so much of his childhood; when this happened, Holck would catch his eyes and give him a meaningful look, and the king would seem to wake up. Holck hoped that these bouts of abstraction were merely a sign of travel-fatigue —

The King who wanted to be a Commoner

Christian had been on the road more than six months – but when he recalled the last years of Frederick the Good, he was inclined to think the worst.

> King Alfonso, who ruled Spain from 1886 to 1931, was so tone deaf that he needed an 'Anthem Man'. Alfonso could not tell one piece of music from another. The job of the Anthem Man was to nudge the king when the national anthem was played so that he knew that he had to stand up.

In early January, 1769, Christian arrived home again. He and the queen were cheered by crowds as they drove into Copenhagen, and that night the town was illuminated. Ministers noted that the king carried himself with more dignity, and now treated the queen with courtly consideration. For a while, the two were reconciled. But those who believed that a leopard can never change its spots pointed out that the king's closest friend was still the dissipated Count Holck, and their predictions proved correct. Within a month or so, the king had slipped back into his old routine of drinking and womanising. He refused to hear a word against Holck – in fact, forced his wife to treat him with respect, and even made her forget protocol and attend Holck's wedding.

Soon it became clear that he had worse problems then debauchery and self-indulgence. He refused to attend to any kind of public business, declined to read papers set in front of him, and could hardly even be persuaded to sign them. Count Holck's fears had been correct – the king was slipping into idiocy. His mind wandered and his conversation became disconnected and sometimes meaningless.

He was not a violent idiot – although he occasionally lost his temper – and there was no need to keep him in restraint. Most of the time, he was simply lethargic and witless – except when out drinking with friends, when he became lively and witless. In effect, Holck became king.

Struensee felt the need to consolidate his power. The king, he decided, needed a mistress – someone who could persuade him to do anything. And Struensee, in turn, needed to be in control of the mistress. He chose an attractive and well-educated woman, Madame de Gabell, whose only drawback was that she was virtuous as well as beautiful. Using all his powers of persuasion, Struensee convinced her that it was her duty to put the good of the country before her own inclinations, and Madame de Gabell finally gave way and surrendered her virtue to the king – as well as to Count Struensee. But the moral conflict caused her such misery that she fell ill and died.

By this time, Struensee had convinced himself that he was in love with the queen. For a year, he used his privilege of being alone with her to make her aware of his feelings. Finally, dancing with him at a court ball, Caroline admitted that she returned his love. The next morning, when they were alone, he suggested reading to her, and after a particularly passionate chapter, seized her in his arms. The queen surrendered, and by the time she left the room, had become his mistress.

Struensee was now created a count, and he and the queen took over the reigns of government. (Christian's step-mother, Juliana, also played an active part.) Meanwhile, Christian remained mildly and pleasantly mad, spending his days drinking and amusing himself – now almost entirely in the palace, because his madness was too obvious to allow him to show himself outside – and at last reconciled to his royal position. In fact, he clung to it – if he showed signs of obstinacy about signing some document, the minister only had to whisper 'Abdication' in his ear to reduce him to obedience.

He still displayed a sense of humour. One day he had been browbeaten into appointing a man he detested to the rank of chamberlain, and when a servant dressed in a yellow vest brought in a pile of wood, the king said: 'I say, how would you like to be a chamberlain?' 'I suppose so', said the man, 'but could you really fix it?' 'Of course. Come with me.' He led the servant into the room where the court was assembled and announced: 'I appoint this man chamberlain of the court.' Since the fiction of the king's sanity had to be maintained, nobody tried to contradict. Later, the Court Marshall had to undo the damage by persuading the man to resign in exchange for a fine estate.

As the king's mind became increasingly blank, Count Holck became bored with the role of boon companion, and left the king to the company of a negro boy and girl, with whom he played games, smashed windows and priceless china, and knocked the heads off statues in the palace gardens.

The queen and Struensee, who had been lovers since 1770, took care to hide it at first, but finally grew careless. The queen, delighted to have someone to love, used to stare at him fondly, and Struensee's acting was equally poor. The affair was soon the scandal of the court, then of Copenhagen. Struensee, after all, was a mere doctor, not even a court official, yet the fact that he and the queen had total control of the king made them the real rulers of the country. The scandal increased when, during a tour of the provinces, the queen chose to dress in men's clothes. The common people were shocked, but the ladies of the court smiled maliciously, waiting for her to make her next mistake.

Struensee, like the queen, was digging his own grave. He was basically a decent man – a liberal, a dreamer of utopian ideals. But he lacked statesmanship and tact. He used his position to abolish the council of state, then went on to introduce some much-needed changes, such as freedom of the press, a responsible judiciary, and municipal reform. It was all very admirable, but he made hundreds of dangerous enemies.

The story of the royal scandal was soon common knowledge. Keith Murray, the British ambassador to Denmark reported the situation to King George III, and as a result the Princess of Wales set out to rescue her daughter from Struensee's clutches. Struensee and the queen heard that she was on her way, and hastened to meet her at Luneborg. When the Princess of Wales attempted to exclude the ever-present Struensee from their conversations by speaking in English, the queen made her own position clear by declaring that she had forgotten the language. The princess had to leave without her daughter.

But the royal families of Europe could not allow the scandal to drag on — this kind of thing encouraged revolutionaries. No matter how mad, Christian would have to be restored. The counter coup was plotted in Denmark itself, by an unlikely conspirator: Queen Juliana-Maria, the king's step mother. Despite her immense dislike of Christian, she knew it was her duty to get rid of the people who were bringing disgrace on the throne. Besides, if Struensee was removed, she would become regent.

On the night of 16 January, 1772, Christian retired at midnight from a masque ball, while the queen and Struensee danced until three in the morning. While Christian was temporarily without a minder, his step-mother and her supporters hastened to the king's bedroom. When he woke up, he was terrified to find them surrounding his bed, Juliana reassured him by falling on her knees, and explaining that there was a conspiracy to assassinate him. She also took the opportunity to tell him — what he probably knew perfectly well — that Struensee was the queen's lover. Juliana had brought a document ordering the arrest of the queen and

The King who wanted to be a Commoner

Struensee, as well as the king's closest companion, a man called Brandt. The feeble-minded king signed it without protest.

Struensee, Brandt and the queen were arrested immediately. At the trial that followed, Struensee and Brandt were found guilty of treason; Brandt was beheaded, and Struensee tortured to death. The queen was found guilty of adultery and her marriage was annulled. George III intervened, and she was removed to Hanover. Shattered by her experience and the death of her lover, she died three years later, at the age of twenty-three.

Christian received no benefit from the coup – he only exchanged one set of manipulators for another. Queen Juliana-Maria and her supporters took control of the country. Christian continued to have flashes of lucidity, as can be seen from a state paper which he signed: 'We, Christian VII, by the grace of God King of Denmark etc, assisted, by the grace of the Devil, by Juliana and Company.'

The Dowager Queen was to rule for only ten years. One day, Christian's teenage son Frederick, who did not inherit his father's weakness of mind, presented at council a warrant that would make him regent during his father's illness. The Queen's retinue were too stunned to protest as they watched the king sign away the country to his son.

The young regent appointed four chamberlains to attend to the amusements of his mad father. Christian lived until 1808, almost into his sixtieth year, when his son Frederick VI became king.

Chapter Four

CHAOS AND SCANDAL IN SERBIA

(I) The Gypsy King

This story begins and ends with a murder.

On 29 May, 1868, Prince Michael of Serbia was out for his evening walk in the deer park at Topchider, near Belgrade, with three female relatives and two servants, when he stopped to exchange greetings with three citizens. As he walked on the citizens shot him in the back, and also opened fire on the others. One lady was killed on the spot, and the others ran away screaming. As Prince Michael lay on the ground, the three assassins came back and repeatedly plunged daggers into his body. They spent so much time making sure he was dead that they were seen by a park keeper, who called the police. The murderers were arrested.

They belonged to the dead prince's main rivals, the Karageorgevich party. Kara George (Black George) was a great Serbian commander who had fought bravely against the Turks in 1804 and driven them out of the country. The Turks returned in 1813 and drove Kara George out of the country. Another commander, Milosh Obren, did better than Black George, and threw the Turks out permanently — although the peace treaty included an agreement to pay them taxes. He became Prince of Serbia. Black George somehow lost his head — it was presented to Prince Milosh

47

in a basket — but his descendants continued to feel that *they* ought to be on the throne of Serbia. Which is why some of them murdered Prince Michael, the descendant of Milosh Obren, in 1868.

The murder threw the Obrenovich supporters into a panic. If the Karageorgevichs moved fast enough, they could seize the throne. At all costs, the death of Prince Michael had to be kept a secret. Fortunately, the assassins had not left their marks on the dead man's face. So his body was placed upright in a carriage, and driven through the streets of Belgrade. Since the assassins were under arrest, their fellow-plotters had no way of knowing that Michael was dead. And when the prince was seen driving through Belgrade, it was assumed that they had failed. In the time they gained, Prince Michael's supporters had time to call Parliament together — it was called the Skupshtina — and have Michael's heir, whose name was Milan, proclaimed Prince.

The Obrenovich supporters heaved a sigh of relief, for it had been a close thing. The problem was that many people felt that Milan had no right to succeed Michael, for he was not Michael's son, or even a very close relative. Prince Michael had been childless, and had no younger brothers or cousins or nephews. But he had searched his memory until he recalled a distant relative named Milan Obren, the son of a man who died of alcoholism and a mother with a reputation for immorality. When Prince Michael located her, she was living in sin with a Rumanian nobleman in his castle, while her neglected son lived among stable boys and gypsies in the filth of the courtyard. Young Milan was half-starved, illiterate and covered with lice. The only time he had revealed anything like royal blood was when he accidentally hanged one of his companions as they played at kings and commoners.

Plucked from the cowdung and horse manure by Prince Michael's messenger, Milan was polished and fumigated

Michael Obrenovitch, Prince of Serbia

before being presented to the prince. Michael liked him, and sent him immediately to Paris to learn to read, write and eat with a knife and fork.

To the disgust of the Karageorgevichs, the people of Belgrade also seemed to like their fourteen year old prince. He had the common touch, and as he grew up, he turned into a fine, manly figure with the bearing of a soldier and a good tempered smile. It was not until he was sent off on a tour of Europe at the age of eighteen that the politicians began to realise that he had his drawbacks, one of which was his assumption that all princes are entitled to spend like millionaires. The bill he ran up on his tour was staggering. Fortunately, Michael had not been a great spender, so when Milan came to the throne, the royal treasury was reasonably well stocked. But at the rate Prince Milan spent, this state of affairs could not last for long. The worried cabinet became almost desperate when one of Milan's first royal decisions was to announce his intention to replace the wooden shacks that then constituted Belgrade with beautiful stone buildings.

These were soon followed by expensive restaurants, nightclubs and gambling establishments. But Milan, while fond of gambling, preferred not to do it in his own capital. He felt it was more aristocratic to lose his money in Budapest, Vienna and Paris. And lose it he did, for he was a singularly unlucky gambler.

As rumours of his losses drifted back to Belgrade, his popularity with his subjects began to dwindle. Hard working peasants can see no reason why their taxes should be thrown away at roulette. Once again, the prince's advisers had to worry about plots to overthrow him and replace him with a descendant of Black George. Fortunately, there was an obvious solution. Nothing improves a prince's popularity so much as marrying a pretty wife and presenting the nation with an heir.

But who would marry an ex-stableboy with an empty treasury? The royal houses of Europe all sent their excuses.

It looked as if Milan would have to be contented with a commoner. He had no objection at all — provided she was rich and physically well-endowed. And when he saw a photograph of a sixteen year old called Natalia Keshko, the daughter of a Russian colonel who owned half of Moldavia, and who was also slim and incredibly beautiful, he lost no time in falling in love with her.

Now oddly enough, Natalie had known she was destined to be a princess for the past ten years. At the age of six, a gypsy fortune teller had looked at her palm, and told her that one day she would wear a queen's crown. (She went on to add the less agreeable information that she would lose it because of something to do with timber.) So when the offer came from Prince Milan of Serbia, Natalie accepted without hesitation, knowing the she was fulfilling at least half of her destiny, for a princess was halfway to becoming a queen.

From the first time they set eyes on her, the people of Belgrade loved her. They were so enthusiastic that they detached her horses from her carriage and pulled it themselves. After that, she was cheered every time she appeared in public. For once, it looked as if Milan had done the right thing.

The marriage itself was held in Vienna, and this again led many Serbs to feel that their prince was letting them down. Traditionally, Serbia allied itself with Russia and against the Austro-Hungarian empire under Emperor Franz Joseph. But then, Franz Joseph was rich enough to make the marriage a sumptuous state occasion, which was more than Milan could afford. The people of Serbia would have their turn to cheer the royal couple at the blessing of the marriage in Belgrade Cathedral.

When the day arrived, the streets around the cathedral were dense with cheering and waving people, prepared to dance and get drunk until late in the evening. The cheers became frenzied as Natalie emerged looking like a fairy princess in cascades of white lace and diamonds. Milan led her to their carriage, gazing at her tenderly. But as they climbed in, something appalling happened. Without warning the sky darkened and there was a mutter of thunder. And when the coachman cracked his whip, the horses ignored him and stood still. Lashing and beating them had no effect. The crowd fell silent — this was clearly the worst kind of omen. When the horses were finally persuaded to move on, the people dispersed in worried silence. That evening the celebrations were subdued.

Yet to begin with, the marriage seemed ideally happy. Milan obviously adored his wife; when one day she said she liked lilies of the valley, he ordered acres of them to be planted. Yet conflicts were already developing. Milan had enormous gambling debts, and he looked forward to paying these off with Natalie's dowry. He was shocked and incredulous when she told him that the dowry was tied up in land investments. He asked her to realize them, and she firmly declined. She had been warned by her relatives that Milan was marrying her for her money, and was quite determined that, if that was the case, he would be disappointed. Milan's original infatuation began to wear thin, particularly when he realised that, in spite of her beauty, Natalie's was a cool and unpassionate nature.

There was another problem. The Serbs were a patriotic people, who were proud of their Slavic nationality, which they shared with Russia. And many patriotic Russians felt that their national identity was being destroyed by the West — Paris and Berlin and Vienna. There was a powerful reaction, known as Pan-Slavism, which was an attempt to restore Slavic pride by turning its back on all things western. Princess Natalie might be a Russian, but she had a French chef and wore elegant western gowns. The Pan-Slavs began to worry in case she corrupted her husband.

Others suspected that he was already corrupted, and they were correct. Milan loved the West; as one who had lived among gypsies and stable lads, he had a healthy dislike of Slav vagueness and incompetence. So when it came to a choice between Russia and Austria, he was willing to choose Austria every time. He took care, of course, not to say so, or the Karageorgevichs would have used it to influence the people against him.

There came a time, in 1876, when he was glad that he had been discreet. The Turks began persecuting Christians in Bulgaria. The Karageorgevichs wanted to know why Serbia was not going to their aid. Milan decided he had better declare war on Turkey. But he lacked the military skills of his ancestor Milosh Obren, and his forces were soon in difficulties. The Pan-Slavs in Russia came to his aid, fought the Russo-Turkish war, and won it. The Serbs celebrated the victory as if it was their own, and for a time, Milan was as popular as any monarch in Europe. His people loved him even more when he and Natalie presented them with an heir to the throne, and named the child Alexander.

But Milan was not entirely happy about the Russian bear and its Slavic enthusiasm – to begin with, the Russians seemed to favour the Bulgarians over the Serbs, and the Serbs had never had the slightest doubt that they were the most important nation in central Europe. This was one belief that Milan shared, and the year after the war against Turkey, he signed a secret treaty with Vienna. It would have cost him his throne if the secret had got out, but Milan was good at keeping secrets. For example, he took care to conceal the fact that, after the birth of the heir, he and Natalie were scarcely on speaking terms. Her refusal to loosen the purse-strings had soured his affections, and he disliked her habit of becoming cool and distant when he did something she disapproved of. Since he was a man who needed a woman to share his bed, he began looking speculatively at the ladies of the court. When she learned of his infidelities, his wife exploded in storms of jealousy that only made things worse. Finally, the hostility between them reached a point where he began to beat her.

She had a minor consolation when, in 1882, Milan proclaimed himself king; at last, the first part of the old gypsy's prophecy had come true, and the commoner's daughter was a queen. But life was still miserable. A kind of cold war had developed between the king and queen. As Natalie made it increasingly clear that the only person she loved was her son, Crown Prince Alexander (known as Sasha), Milan's response was to womanise with increased abandon. He also expressed his disgust with his queen in small but hurtful ways, such as spitting tobacco juice on her beautiful white carpets.

Even in his infidelities he was accident-prone. In Vienna, he began a liaison with a famous actress, and presented her with a photograph of himself set in gold and diamonds. She replied, thanking him for the picture, and explaining that her gratitude would have been even deeper had the diamonds been real. The picture and its frame were returned with the note. Astonished, Milan had the stones tested, and was bewildered when they proved to false. To make amends, he presented the actress with another jewel, this time an indisputably real one. Many years later he discovered the truth. Passing a Viennese jeweller's shop, Milan noticed a frame of the same design for sale in the window. Enquiring within, he learnt that the jeweller had copied the frame from one that he had handled years before. An actress had brought it in, asking him to replace the diamonds in it with fakes.

Now she was queen, Natalie recalled gloomily the second part of the gypsy's prophecy — that she would lose her crown through something to do with timber. As she drove through woods, she always watched carefully in case any overhanging branch looked ready to snap off in the wind.

In fact, her nemesis proved to be a woman named Artemisia Christich, who was the daughter of a timber merchant. She was the wife of Milan's private secretary, and soon became the king's mistress. Unlike Natalie, Artemisia was more typically Slav – with large black eyes, masses of dark hair, and a full and heavy-breasted figure. She was several years Milan's senior, but he did not care – she gave him the kind of admiration he craved, and treated him with motherly tenderness. The king was so besotted with her that many of his courtiers thought he was bewitched. When she bore him a child, her husband obligingly divorced her.

And now, to the horror of his ministers, Milan began to talk about divorcing his wife. No one had any doubt that he was thinking of marrying Artemisia. His advisers pointed out to him that he had no grounds for divorcing Natalie. She had not been unfaithful, nor was likely to be – she was far too prudish.

The king considered the point, and talked it over with his mistress. It seemed intolerable to them both that he should be saddled with a woman he hated, and unable to live openly with the woman he loved. Finally, Milan hit upon a cunning solution. His son was now eleven – time he began to see more of the world. His mother adored him so much that the idea of abandoning him to strangers would arouse all her possessiveness. So why should she not accompany him on his travels?

Just as he expected, Natalie accepted with enthusiasm. Soon, she and Sasha were living in Wiesbaden. Once she was out of the country, the king heaved a sigh of relief, and vowed that she would never return. It was some time before the queen began to suspect that this was her husband's intention. She began to write friendly letters, but it was too late. One morning in June 1888, she received a letter from Milan informing her that he intended to have the marriage dissolved. Soon after that, he told her that he wanted the Crown Prince returned to Belgrade – alone.

Royal Scandals

> The mad Roman emperor Caligula made his
> horse, Incitatus, a consul. The animal would dine
> with the emperor at banquets. Even after
> Caligula was assassinated, and his uncle Claudius
> became emperor, the horse retained its
> position.

Years of living with her husband's infidelities had made
Natalie good at one thing – protesting. Now she did it at
the top of her voice, and turned herself into a *cause celebre*.
Milan ignored the storm, and had his son dragged away
from her by force. Natalie was in agony; she had no doubt
that Sasha would be poisoned by the king's mistress, and
that he would then marry her, making her own son – Obren
– the heir to the throne.

But if that was Artemisia's intention, she had no time to
carry it out. The divorce – granted by the Orthodox
Church – scandalized the country. Serbs were old fashioned, and Milan's behaviour seemed unforgivable. Artemisia became so unpopular that she was afraid to show her
face in the street.

In the face of this storm, Milan had a flash of inspiration.
The answer was simple: to abdicate in favour of his son.
Being king had brought him nothing but misery. But if he
abdicated, it would solve all his problems at a single sweep.
His enemies would stop trying to kill him (he had survived
a number of attempts on his life), and they would certainly
not be unsporting enough to assassinate a child. He could
live as a private citizen in the capitals of Europe on a royal
pension, and finally enjoy life.

He overruled the frantic protests of his ministers, who
felt that he was abandoning them to the Karageorevichs,
and on 22 March, 1889, made his abdication speech. Oddly
enough, those who heard it declared that it was not the

56

king's voice, and it confirmed the opinion of many of them
that Artemisia was a witch, who had somehow cast a spell
on the king and made him her puppet.

If that was true, she was to receive a shock. As soon as he
ceased to be king, he hastened back to Vienna and his other
favourite capitals, and flung himself into the kind of life he
had not enjoyed since he was eighteen. Artemisia pursued
him for a while, complaining pitifully, and trying to blackmail him with his love letters, but it was no good. Milan had
decided in favour of freedom from responsibility, and that
included Artemisia.

(2) The King and the Commoner

In the story of the Obrenovichs, the supernatural makes a
number of curious incursions. One of these had occurred on
the day Prince Michael was murdered, 29 May, 1868. In a
market town named Ujitsa, an old peasant named Matha
ran down the street shouting: 'Help! They are murdering
our prince!' He was under arrest when a telegram arrived
from Belgrade, announcing Prince Michael's murder. Inevitably, Matha became a suspect. Yet a little interrogation
convinced the police that he was just a simple peasant, who
was unlikely to be a conspirator. Moreover, his neighbours
all confirmed that he often had flashes of clairvoyance
which proved accurate.

The police now asked him if he had any other prophecies
for the future, and Matha proceeded, in the presence of the
mayor, to predict the destiny of Serbia for a long time to
come. All of this was written down by the mayor's
secretary. The lengthy statement – which became known
as the Black Prophecy – was placed in the local court
archives. It included the comment that King Milan would
one day abdicate. About Milan's successor it had rather
more sinister things to say.

So had a clairvoyant in Paris, a certain Madame de Thebes. One day, the ex-queen Natalie visited the clairvoyant, together with her faithful maid and companion, Draga Mashin, a bosomy lady past the first flush of youth, but with a gentle manner that Natalie found appealing. The clairvoyant began by telling Natalie that she was nourishing a viper in her bosom, a statement the ex-queen found incomprehensible.

Draga then asked about her own future. The clairvoyant replied: 'You will marry the highest in the land, but you will ruin him. You will die together.'

All this sounded so absurd that the two women decided that they had caught Madame de Thebes on one of her off-days, and thought no more about it.

Since Draga Mashin will play a central part in this story, it is necessary to explain who she was. Her grandfather had ruined himself by lending money to Serbia's saviour, Milosh Obren, and the family had fallen on hard times. Draga's father went insane, and a husband Draga married at 17, died of drink. Her husband's brother, Alexander Mashin, seems to have suspected that Draga had poisoned her husband — at all events, he had some reason for not merely disliking her, but hating her. Over the next year or so, Draga, who was slim and pretty, took a number of lovers, but ended as poor as ever. It was then that her plight was drawn to the attention of the charitable and philanthropic Natalie, who took her in and made her a Lady in Waiting. Dragas's loyalty was so total and obvious that Natalie did not even suspect that she might be the viper referred to by Madame de Thebes. And the notion that Draga might marry her son and bring about the end of the dynasty would have struck her as too absurd to contemplate.

But now Sasha was heir to the throne, and Milan was far away in some gambling resort or other, Natalie found herself wondering whether it was not time she returned home. Her twelve year old son was now without a father or mother, and there were rumours that the guardian appointed by ex-King Milan treated the child harshly. Jovan Ristich was only one of three regents, but since he was the ex-premier of Serbia, was by far the most important. It was to him that Natalie now wrote asking permission to return to Belgrade.

His reply was an irritable refusal. He and his two fellow guardians had sworn, he said, that Natalie would not be allowed near her son. But Natalie was a determined woman. She announced that, whether Ristich liked it or not, she was returning home. No one, she said, had a right to keep a mother and her only child apart.

She carried out her threat, and as cheering peasants lined the river bank to wave at her steamer, Ristich realised that he had a formidable rival. It was obvious that if Natalie could establish herself in Belgrade, she would soon replace him as regent.

Natalie arrived at the palace, and found the gates locked and guarded. The crowd shouted angrily, but the guards refused to open. Natalie was forced to go away, and find herself a house on nearby Prince Michael Street. Every day she returned to the palace and stared at the facade, wondering if Sasha was looking out of a window at her. And the crowd that gathered round her continued to treat her as their rightful queen. Ristich was suddenly the most unpopular man in Belgrade.

Clearly, he was in an impossible position. Finally, he telegraphed the king, begging him to allow Prince Sasha to meet his mother. Milan telegraphed back, with resigned disgust, giving permission. Natalie was finally allowed into the palace, where Sasha flung himself into her arms. He was a rather short, ugly boy with a bullet-head and glasses, and the last time he had received any affection was when he was in Wiesbaden with his mother. Now he was overjoyed to see her again.

Ristich's misgivings were justified. The ex-queen was not content to see her son regularly and give him affection. She soon began to show flashes of the old imperiousness that had alienated her husband. She encouraged Sasha's dislike of his guardians, and gave interviews to newspapers — who loved 'human' stories than as much as they do today — about the injustices she had borne. Within a few months she was more of an embarrassment than ever.

Ristich asked her to leave, and she ignored him. He had a decree of banishment passed, and she ignored that too. Finally, Ristich played his last card. He used his tremendous authority as a guardian to force Prince Sasha to read the decree of banishment to his mother, and to beg her to obey Parliament. Natalie left the palace with a stony face. She was determined to stay where she was.

Soon after, the police arrived at Prince Michael Street while Natalie was still in her night clothes. She demanded to be allowed to say goodbye to her friends, and spent several hours embracing them. Finally, the police seized her and frog-marched her to her carriage. By now the street was crowded with a sympathetic populace, who booed the police and cheered when Natalie's friends tried to attack them. As Natalie was forced into the carriage, a miniature revolution broke loose. Men grasped the wheels of the carriage, others held the horses, and Natalie was taken out of the door on the other side. The police were forced to use their rifle butts to fight their way through to her. As the carriage moved on, the mood of the crowd grew ugly, and they began throwing things at the escort. Their numbers swelled, and the police realised that they could only gain control by opening fire — which might start a real revolution. So when the carriage once more came to a halt in the noisy throng, they made no attempt to resist as the horses were removed from the shafts, and strong peasants drew the queen back to her house in Prince Michael Street. The rioting went on until dark, and a number of people were killed.

Ristich and his fellow ministers were furious but worried; it began to look as the queen was going to remain by popular demand. Somehow, the situation had to be resolved before it became dangerous. That night, soldiers climbed over the rooftops, and down into the courtyard of Natalie's house. They were relieved to find that Natalie's escort of sturdy pleasants had gone home, convinced their queen was safe. Natalie – and her Lady in Waiting – were taken swiftly to the station in a cab, and when Belgrade awoke the next morning, they were far away.

The Skupshtina passed another bill, banning her from ever setting foot in Serbia. For good measure, they also banned Milan. Unlike the ex-queen, the ex-king was perfectly happy to hear the news. He was a pensioner of the Serbian government, and they now added a gift of a million francs in exchange for his promise to stay out of the country.

For Prince Sasha, the next few years were heartbreaking. Surrounded by spies, whose job was to make sure that he was not in secret contact with his mother, he spent his days like a prisoner. Only one person sympathized – his French tutor. He shared the French taste for liberal politics, and felt that Serbia under Ristich was a prison. Therefore he sympathized with those who wanted to see the downfall of the present government. The tutor agreed to establish contact between the banished ex-king and queen and their unhappy son, and since he often travelled back to France, he found this easy. King Milan and Queen Natalie usually had nothing but detestation for one another, but at the moment, neither had anything to lose by plotting to overthrow Ristich and his cronies. If Ristich was overthrown, they might be allowed access to their son – and the royal treasury.

On 12 April, 1893, Prince Sasha invited all his ministers and generals to dine with him. They were puzzled, but agreed. Finally, after the toasts, the king stood up to address them. After a few minutes, the smiles vanished from their faces. Prince Alexander was announcing that, at sixteen, he felt that he had come of age, and would assume his role as the King of Serbia. The ministers and generals, he explained, would remain there in the palace as his 'guests'.

A general tried to leave the room, and found armed soldiers outside the door. Other doors opened, and soldiers with bayonets entered the room. Ristich, who was summoning all his authority to suppress his rebellious ward, recognized that he was beaten, and sat down with a stunned expression.

The people of Belgrade woke up to the news that Ristich was no longer in power, and that their new king was Prince Sasha. They were delighted, and their approval increased when Alexander announced his new cabinet. The old guard, that had been struggling so obviously for the past years, was banished. Instead the Radical party had overall control. This seemed to be a signal that the unpopular pro-European ways of the old king had been abandoned in favour of the 'Slavonic Cause' and the 'Serbian Dream'. Certainly the new government was pro-Russian, and this in itself delighted the people. But Europe also approved the coup, for it seemed both amusing and romantic — like Anthony Hope's recent bestseller *The Prisoner of Zenda*.

The Karageorgevichs, who were behind the coup, were also well-pleased. They were now the government instead of the opposition. And although the prince was an Obrenovich, he was only a child. That problem could wait.

What they feared, of course, was that the honeymoon would continue, and that King Alexander would become as popular as his mother — in which case, they would be no better off than before. What they hoped was that he might do something so stupid that the people would be anxious to see the last of him. In due course, Sasha would oblige them.

The stage was set for tragedy. Sasha's difficult life had made him mistrustful. Lack of affection had made him unemotional. He struck people as a cold fish, awkward and withdrawn. His father had at least been a loveable rogue; by comparison, Sasha seemed dull, commonplace and too self-controlled.

One of his first decisions was to go and visit his mother in Biarritz, where Natalie had set up a kind of miniature court. She had covered the walls of her house with pictures of her son, and named it 'Sashino' or Little Sasha's House. She was naturally overjoyed at the thought of being reunited with her long-lost darling, of watching him relax and expand in the warm sunshine and pleasant company of Biarritz. Everyone wanted to meet him, including the crowds of children, sons and daughters of Rumanian nobles, with whom Natalie had filled her house – for their admiration reminded her of the crowds who cheered her in Belgrade. Moreover, every hostess in Biarritz wanted to give a party for King Alexander.

As soon as she saw him again, Natalie knew that it was not to be. Sasha was an awkward adolescent, and his appearance was unimpressive. He was small and dark, and the tight set of his mouth gave him a sulky expression, while the round glasses made him look like an owl. His manners were stiff and formal, and he seemed to be worried in case smiling caused his face to crack. Natalie, of course, knew that this coldness concealed a lonely child who longed for affection; but others were taken in by the appearance, and reacted accordingly. The children behaved with the natural cruelty of the young and confident; they closed ranks against him.

So King Sasha soon came to accept that he was a social failure. Like any unhappy adolescent, he withdrew into himself. Their was only one person with whom he felt completely at ease – his mother's homely and friendly Lady in Waiting, Draga Mashin. It was Draga's job to superintend the children on the beach, where she sat under her umbrella reading a popular novel or gazing at the sea. Sasha found that he preferred to join her, for she was the one person in Biarritz with whom he felt truly at ease.

In spite of the clairvoyant's prophecy, Natalie had no suspicion that there could be anything to worry her about the relationship. How could she possibly believe that this awkward adolescent would fall in love with a woman twice his age? Later she was blamed for not separating them, yet the whole idea of their having an affair would have struck her as absurd.

Yet it was true. Alexander's liking for the soft and motherly Draga had soon turned to love. At this stage she regarded him as a child, towards whom she felt merely protective. But a dangerous incident was to bring them closer together. Despite his natural distaste for physical activities, Sasha enjoyed swimming, which he had learned in secret while under the guardianship of the joyless Ristich. He enjoyed demonstrating his new skill in front of Draga, and would plunge into the water and swim up and down the beach, periodically smiling and waving at her. He made light of the warnings that when the tide changed, the current could have a powerful undertow, for he had complete trust in his baigneur (or minder), a Basque sailor who could swim like an otter.

One day, as he and his minder were swimming in a rough sea, an unusually large wave plunged them both under the water. Draga screamed, and the children ceased their game. After a long, nerve-wracking pause, Alexander surfaced, and was cast up on the beach by another huge wave. But the Basque sailor failed to reappear, and his body floated ashore some hours later. The death was seen as a bad omen, although what it presaged no one was sure.

From Biarritz and Draga, Alexander reluctantly detached himself to visit his father in Paris. The entertainments favoured by Milan were quite unlike the drawing rooms of Biarritz. The ex-king felt that his son needed educating in the ways of the world, and proceeded to introduce him to

Parisian music halls, gambling establishments and brothels. Milan, like Natalie, found his son's appearance disappointing, and Sasha's lack of enthusiasm for actresses led him to suspect that the boy was either paralysingly shy or impotent. He had no way of knowing that Alexander had left his heart behind in Biarritz.

Alexander worked out a cunning solution to this problem. Feeling that he now had the right to interfere in the wranglings of his parents, through which he had sat, agonized and powerless, throughout so much of his childhood, the new king declared their divorce null and void. Milan had no objection to this arrangement, for although he detested his ex-wife, re-marriage might allow him access to her fortune. Natalie also had no objection, because with the ending of the divorce came the ending of her exile – as the wife of the former king, she could now return to Belgrade as the queen-mother, rather than as a rejected spouse. Alexander was equally satisfied, since his mother's retinue included her Lady in Waiting.

And so Natalie finally had her hands on what she dreamed about. She was, in effect, the ruler of Serbia. Her son was more interested in the plump figure at his mother's side than in opposing her political suggestions. Natalie was so happy that she failed to notice this. With a group of friends – who became known as 'the tea time parliament' – she held her own cabinet meetings and decided what was best for the country. And her son nodded, and accepted everything she said.

Milan decided not to return to Belgrade – he greatly preferred Paris. Instead, he encouraged his son to visit him as often as possible, and enjoyed treating him man-to-man, and showing him the delights of real civilization.

It could not last. Alexander's new cabinet – the real one – was already hard enough to deal with; these middle-aged politicians, still enjoying the sensation of power, were inclined to treat the teenage king as a rubber stamp. And now he was once again allowing himself to be influenced by his mother and father, they were furious. They criticized him, bullied him, and often shouted at him. Alexander hated violence, and his resentment increased. Finally, recollecting that he was king, he rescinded the liberal constitution that had been his father's abdication gift to his people, and replaced it with the old one. This in turn gave him enough power to impose his will on his cabinet. Since he had now been king for four years, he was at last beginning to acquire the political skills to handle rebellious advisers.

Yet his common sense also made him aware that it would be suicidal to allow his enemies to say that Serbia was run by a petticoat government. He explained the situation to his mother, and she agreed that it made sense. Reluctantly, she returned to Biarritz. Draga, of course, went with her.

· And it may have been this latest separation from the king that led Draga, at last, to grant him the favours he had been begging for the past three years. For it was on a visit to his mother at Biarritz that Sasha and Draga finally became lovers. A friendly minister to whom the king later poured out his heart was surprised to learn that Draga had not surrendered her virtue on that original visit to Biarritz, nor even after she had moved back to Belgrade. The king described an occasion when he had leapt upon her from a cupboard while staying at Sashino, and how Draga had fought him off, grabbed him by the collar, and put him firmly out of the room, locking the door behind him. He tried again and again, but Draga remained firm — even when, in Belgrade, her suitor was now her king and could — in theory — command her. But in 1896, when she finally acknowledged that she loved him and surrendered her body, Alexander experienced the first taste of real happiness in his life.

At first they kept their secret well — they were both aware of the scandal that disclosure would cause. But when he was back in Belgrade, the king poured out his loneliness in daily love letters. At first, since the queen suspected nothing, Draga was able to hide these from her mistress. But one day the inevitable happened, and one of the letters fell into Natalie's hands.

Her fury was unbounded. A love affair between her son and this . . . inferior creature was unthinkable. There may also have been an element of jealousy present, for a possessive mother sees her son with the eyes of a lover. At any rate, convinced that her sense of shock was due to the fact that her son was engaged in a sexual relationship outside marriage, she gave way to her outrage and ordered Draga to pack her bags immediately. Then she did her best to make sure that Draga starved to death by writing letters to anyone who might offer help, describing how Draga had betrayed her trust.

Draga was shattered. She had no savings, for her family was extended and poverty-stricken, and her generous salary as Lady in Waiting had been distributed among them. Now she had not only lost her own livelihood but that of her dependents. There was — as Natalie should have realized — only one place she could go: Belgrade.

For Alexander it was a dream come true. He swept her into his arms, cradled her head, and listened to her tearful story. Of course, he told her, her family would be looked after. For love of him she had lost her livelihood, now it was only fair that he should recompense her. He installed her in a house on Crown Street, near the palace, and placed funds at her disposal. Then he took her off for a winter holiday in the Tyrol — which was, in effect, their honeymoon.

Too late Natalie recogized that she was to blame. As the rumour spread that her ex-servant was now the Serbian royal mistress, she must have been tormented with point-less regrets and suspicions. Had Alexander's frequent visits to Biarritz been to see his beloved mother or her beloved maid? The answer was soon clear. By dismissing Draga, Natalie had also dismissed her son. She never saw him again.

Perhaps to make her feel worse, Alexander now invited his father to return to Belgrade to reorganize the army. Milan accepted with gratitude – for as usual, he was broke. The appointment caused widespread criticism, since Milan was remembered as a playboy who squandered the country's taxes in foreign casinos. In fact, Milan surprised everybody by proving to be a highly efficient commander. Recognizing that the chief threat to the throne was a disaffected army, he organised a decree that made sure that his soldiers were paid on time, then set about drilling them until they looked less like a stage chorus from a comic opera. After that, Milan settled back into the easy life, only slightly regretting that Belgrade was not Paris.

And now, with that infallible talent for doing the wrong thing, he began to dabble once more in politics. Unlike both the Obrenovichs and the Karageorgevichs, Milan was what would now be called a good European. He had no patience with the 'Serbian dream' and politicians who preferred Moscow to Vienna. Beside, his best hope of future reward – if he should have to return to exile – was to gain favour with Emperor Franz Joseph of Austria. A few years earlier he had been widely execrated when newspapers published details of his secret treaty with Austria, but at that time Milan had been safely in Paris. Now he was plotting again to get rid of the Slavophiles and Russophiles, and even the rumours caused his son's enemies to grind their teeth.

But it was his next scheme that began the slide to disaster. For it now struck Milan that the simplest way of breaking the power of the Russophiles was to persuade his son to marry a German – or Austrian – princess, who would exert her influence to make him favour his European allies.

This was not the first time that the idea of a politically advantageous marriage had been raised; Natalie, during her short stay in Belgrade, had summoned several beautiful Slavic women of noble birth and presented them to

Alexander in turn. To each he had succeeded in making himself objectionable. And when he was little more than a boy, radical politicians had taken him to Montenegro and tried to force him to marry a Serbian princess, but Sasha had resisted so violently that the idea had to be abandoned.

His reaction was just as violent now his father wanted him to marry a German. He was in love with Draga, and was determined that she would remain his queen — at least in the privacy of her little house in Crown Street. It was obviously out of the question to marry Draga, but he saw no reason why he should be forced to marry anyone else.

Kingship had taught him cunning. He appeared to take his father's suggestion seriously, and declared himself perfectly willing to marry a princess who was beautiful, intelligent and wealthy. This led Milan to recall his own humiliating attempt to find himself a royal bride, and to recognize that it might not be such a good idea after all.

But it had implanted in Sasha's mind the recognition that if he was not to be forced to marry some Wagnerian blonde with a Prussian accent, he had better stage a pre-emptive strike. After all, he *was* the king, and two previous bids to assert his authority had been successful. Why should he not marry the woman he loved?

There were others who said that the idea of marrying Draga had been planted in the king's head in a quite different way — by witchcraft. One of Draga's friends was a Rumanian lady of common origin, who was now married to a Russian general. She told Draga that she had been her husband's mistress for years when she had dropped a love potion — supplied by a local witch — into his tea. Soon after that, the general had proposed. Following the witch's instructions, the lady had refused him seven times, then accepted him. Now the lady offered to obtain the same potion for Draga . . .

We do not know whether she accepted it. What we do know is that Draga, who had accustomed herself to the idea that her lover would have to marry someone of his own station, now began to wonder whether it *was* inevitable. Conspiracy theorists have even suggested that the Rumanian lady was planted in Belgrade by the Russian intelligence service, and that her task was to turn Draga's thoughts towards becoming queen – and so make King Alexander the most unpopular man in Serbia . . .

It was at about this time that Milan's envoys announced that they were close to accomplishing their mission of finding a German princess who would be willing to become queen of Serbia. Alexander began to feel more and more like a hunted hare.

The people of Belgrade could hardly help noticing that Draga was the king's mistress. He slept at her house every night and was taken away by a carriage early in the morning. This situation brought unpleasant echoes of an earlier royal love affair – between Milan and Artemesia Cristich. To Serbian patriots, it seemed almost incredible that their new king had also fallen pray to the witchcraft of another plump and homely schemer.

But now a German princess had been found, help was in sight. So ex-king Milan, aided by the Prime Minister Dr Georgevich, spurred themselves on for a final effort.

Incredibly, Alexander appeared to capitulate. He sent for his father and Dr Georgevich and told them that he had decided to follow their advice and marry the princess. But since both looked exhausted, they should first take a holiday. And when they returned, the king would be ready to go with them to meet his prospective bride.

This, they suspected, was his final struggle. He had realised that there was nothing to stop him marrying a princess *and* keeping Draga as a mistress. Reassured, both agreed to go and recuperate abroad – Milan to Carlsbad, Dr Georgevich to Marienbad.

A month later came the bombshell – a coded message from Georgevich's deputy in Belgrade, telling him that a dreadful misfortune was about to fall upon Serbia. This took some time to decode, because the king had arranged for them to be supplied with the wrong codebooks. But direct contact with Belgrade finally established the nature of the misfortune: the king had announced that he was going to marry Draga.

Georgevich telegraphed Alexander to ask him if this was true; when the king said yes, Georgevich resigned.

Milan sent his son a shocked letter: 'Nothing remains for me but to pray to God for our fatherland. I shall be the first to cheer the government which shall drive you from the country after such folly — Your father, Milan.' The order of banishment against Milan was renewed as soon as Alexander received this letter, and all payments to him from the privy purse were stopped. Milan died penniless a year later at the age of forty-seven.

The first Ming emperor of China, Hung Wu, was very afraid of the earthbound soul of his Yuan dynasty predecessor. Hung Wu believed that the former emperor's vital force lived in Peiping, the Yuan emperor's capital. To rid himself of the malign spirit, Hung Wu commanded that Peiping be completely destroyed. Before his army carried out the order, Hung Wu had historians record the beauty of the city's palace.

In Belgrade, the king was meeting stiff opposition; ministers begged him to reconsider, and some were even bold enough to refer to Draga as a lady of ill fame. With tears in his eyes, the king declared that she was the most honourable woman he had ever known, and that she had repeatedly refused to marry him. He was simply unable to understand why people tried to drag her name in the mud.

The ministers approached Draga and begged her to leave the country and save the king from ruin. She seemed moved by their arguments, and agreed. She left the house in Crown Street, climbed into her carriage, and told the ministers that she would stay with a friend until preparations had been made for her to leave the country. Yet within hours, the king knew where she was staying, and had her brought to the palace. Then he made the public announcement that he intended to marry her.

He should have suspected something when he received a telegram of congratulation from the tsar of Russia, Nicholas II, offering to act as best man – for the tsar had every reason to want to see Alexander dethroned in favour of a pro-Russian Karageorgevich. Instead, Alexander took the message at its face value, and was encouraged to press on – as the tsar hoped he would. Like every other Slavophile, he was delighted to see Alexander conniving at his own destruction.

The wedding in Belgrade Cathedral was magnificent; the king was determined to show everyone that he regarded Draga as the most beautiful and eligible princess in Europe. The Russian ambassador stood in as proxy for Tsar Nicholas, who, for 'reasons of state', was unable to attend. For all its pomp and ceremony, the wedding failed to arouse the people of Belgrade out of their resigned apathy.

When Draga announced shortly afterwards that she was pregnant, Alexander hoped that his people would at last open their hearts to her. He was unaware that his mother had sent dozens of postcards to friends in Belgrade telling them that her former Lady in Waiting had long ago had an operation that had made her infertile. This rumour was already widespread even before Draga announced her pregnancy. And when it was noted that Draga's sister was also pregnant, the conclusion seemed obvious: the king meant to foist an imposter on the Serbian people.

The gossip soon reached the ears of the tsar. As best man, it was also his duty to stand godfather to the first child. Understandably, Nicholas was seized by misgivings — he had no intention of causing himself future embarrassment by standing godfather to an imposter. So he sent two of his own doctors to examine Queen Draga.

The news, when it came, seemed to confirm everyone's suspicions. Draga was not pregnant, and never had been. In an attempt to save her embarrassment, the doctors pointed out that Draga was suffering from a gynecological condition that could have made her believe that she was going to have a baby. No one believed them.

In 1903 there was rioting in Belgrade and the rioters were shot down in the street. In March the constitution was suspended for a short time, and certain judges were dismissed. Then Alexander committed his final act of folly by nominating Draga's brother Nikodiye as his heir. This time, even the cabinet — packed with the king's supporters — was shocked. They went to confront the king, and the Prime Minister asked Draga to withdraw. She refused. When a general told the king that there would be a revolution if he adopted Nokodiye as his heir, he replied: 'I am the king and I shall do as I please.' Draga added: 'The king's word is supreme.' And so the meeting broke up.

All this made a coup inevitable. The notion of getting rid of Alexander and placing a Kerageorgevich on the throne became a topic for discussion not only in obscure bars, but in open streets and parks and squares. The leader of the conspirators was Draga's brother-in-law, Colonel Alexander Mashin — the man who suspected her of poisoning her first husband, and who now had new reason for resentment since he had been placed on the retired list.

Perhaps aware that nothing that they did could make them more unpopular, the unhappy couple appointed as many of Draga's relatives as they could find to high positions in the army. As in-laws of the king, these new officers insisted upon greater respect than their fellows – for example, that the orchestra should play the national anthem when they entered a theatre.

At this point in this story, the supernatural makes yet another incursion. On 20 March, 1903, the London editor W.T. Stead brought together a group of people in Gatti's Restaurant. The aim was to introduce them to a 'spirit medium' from Bradford, a Mrs Burchell. At a session in the afternoon, Mrs Burchell's attempts to display her powers had been unsuccessful, but after dinner, feeling more relaxed, she was asked to try again. Mrs Burchell was known for her success in 'psychometry', the ability to hold some object and sense its history. Stead now placed in her hand an envelope he had obtained from the Serbian ambassador, Mr Chedomille Mijatovich, and asked her if she received any impressions. The envelope contained a signature of King Alexander.

Mrs Burchell said instantly: 'Royalty! He is a king.' She then gave an accurate description of Alexander, becoming increasingly agitated. 'He will be murdered in his palace, together with his queen. Men will rush into his chamber and shoot him. The queen implores them to spare his life, but they kill her too . . .'

Another medium in the room had also fallen into a trance, and added the detail that the uniforms of the murderers looked to her like Russian uniforms.

Stead wrote a full account of the seance, and sent it to the Serbian ambassador, who forwarded it to King Alexander. But Alexander was a rationalist who regarded clairvoyants as fakes, and ignored the warning . . .

In Belgrade, the plot gathered pace. The first plan was to shoot the king and queen as they left a concert; this had to be abandoned because crowds pressed around them when the moment came to fire. This is why the conspirators finally decided to kill them in the palace. The date chosen was 10 June, 1903, the anniversary of the assassination of

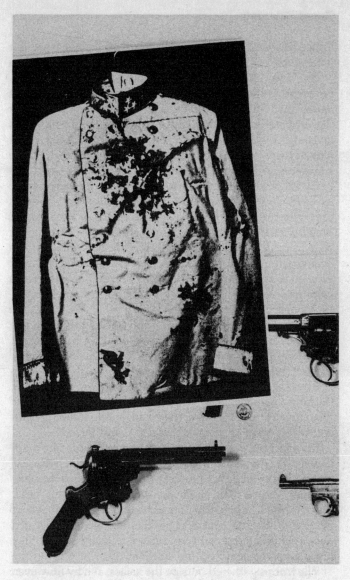

The assassination guns and jacket in which King Alexandra I was murdered

Prince Michael. Alexander and Draga had been married for three years.

By June 1903, the king and his wife were virtually prisoners in the palace. Aware that they were universally hated, their main hope was that the support of Mother Russia would deter any attempt on their lives. The Russian Embassy was full of the tsar's troops, and it was to these, rather than to the untrustworthy Serbian army, that Alexander looked in the event of a crisis.

Alexander had grown to hate his people as much as they hated him, which meant that the conspirators had nothing to fear from their fellow countrymen. The coup was delayed only by a lack of unanimity about whether the king should be murdered or merely forced to abdicate. So the date of the anniversary of the assassination of Prince Michael was allowed to pass. It was on 16 June, 1903, that all differences were resolved, and Draga's ex-brother-in-law gave orders to put the plan into action.

The night was hot and sticky, too hot to sleep, and the people of Belgrade were sitting out drinking in pavement cafes and beer gardens. Almost everybody seemed to know that something was about to happen.

The king's equerry Nauomovich had the task of drugging the king's personal bodyguard, a group of men selected for their loyalty. By the time they had drunk Nauomovich's wine, they were all ready to lie down and sleep it off.

Mashin now called upon another conspirator, the commander of Alexander's own infantry regiment, who explained to his men that the king had ordered them to obey Colonel Mashin. The regiment, with Mashin at its head, was cheered by citizens as it marched through the streets of Belgrade. The police, at first puzzled and alarmed, decided not to act. They had not been invited to take part, but they knew when to stand on the sidelines . . .

The troops gathered outside the palace, and by now even those who had not been told must have guessed what was about to happen. Draga was awakened by the sounds of the men in the courtyard. Having expected just such sounds for years, she leapt out of bed, roused her husband, and together they hid in a concealed closet.

The keys to the gate had been stolen from the drugged commander of the king's bodyguard; the palace was thrown open to the conspirators. The guard on duty was shot dead as he challenged them. Hearing the noise, Laza, the king's aide-de-camp, came to investigate. He too was shot, although not fatally. The soldiers then began smashing down the palace doors, searching for the king and queen. After an hour ransacking the rooms, they had still failed to find their quarry.

In the Russian embassy, the ambassador watched the proceedings from a high window. The palace windows, mostly in darkness, were lit occasionally by flashes of gunfire as soldiers fired their weapons into closets and beds. He had been told what going to happen, and had silently acquiesced.

Infuriated by their failure to find the king, the soldiers began to torture Laza. He tried to gain time by suggesting that they should search the new palace, an extension that Alexander had ordered in the palace courtyard. At that point Mashin arrived on the scene, and told them not to waste their time.

Drunk and demoralized, the conspirators were on the point of abandoning the plot when the queen gave them the clue that they needed. Both she and Alexander had by now been huddled in the dark for over two hours. They had no idea who was destroying the palace, but were disinclined to believe that it could be the army. Then Draga, who seemed born to do the wrong thing, peered out of the closet's small window, saw the troops in the courtyard, and thought they were loyal soldiers coming to the rescue. She shouted at them to come quickly, for the king was about to be murdered. Recognizing her voice, the army started shooting. Draga was not hit; she dived back into the room. But now the soldiers knew where she was.

Crashing upstairs, dragging the bleeding Laza along with them, Mashin and his men slashed the already damaged bedroom to pieces. Yet they were still unable to find the concealed closet. As soldiers hacked at the walls with axes, Mashin assured Laza that they had no intention of harming the king — merely of forcing his abdication.

'Do you swear that is true?'

'I swear.' He showed Laza a document of abdication that he had brought with him.

'You promise not to harm the king?'

'You have my word of honour.'

Laza knocked at a certain spot on the wall, and the door opened. Another of the conspirators, Colonel Mischich, ran forward and fired at the king, who fell. Then as the queen ran forward to support her husband, Mashin pushed Mischich aside, and fired at her. He missed. Another officer fired, and she fell. As the bodies lay on the floor, the officers emptied their revolvers into them, then hacked them with their swords.

Finally they lifted the mutilated and almost naked body of the queen, and hurled her out of the window into the garden. The soldiers below cheered. But when the assassins tried to hurl the king after her, Alexander suddenly came to life, and grabbed the window frame. A sword cut off his fingers, and he was thrown out.

Elsewhere in the palace, soldiers loyal to the king were murdered, including Laza. Nauomovich was somehow killed in the confusion. Draga's two brothers were seized in their houses and executed; the three soldiers ordered to kill them at first refused, and were shot themselves. All over Belgrade, supporters of the Obrenovichs were killed.

The massacres would have continued if it had not been for the Austro-Hungarian minister, who informed Mashin that unless the murders ceased, the Austrian army would cross the Danube and occupy Belgrade. But he was too late to save the Austro-Serbian alliance. Peter, the Karageorge pretender to the Serbian throne, arrived from exile in Geneva soon afterwards. On 19 June, in a ceremony at which the head of the Serbian church thanked the army for its patriotism, Peter Karageorgevich was crowned king of Serbia.

Chapter Five

THE MAYERLING AFFAIR

The suicide of Archduke Rudolf of Habsburg after killing his eighteen year old mistress has been described as the greatest royal scandal of modern times.

If Rudolf had lived, he would have presided over a collapsing empire. The dynasty of the Habsburgs had dominated Europe for seven hundred years. But by the end of the nineteenth century, it had spread itself too far; it had too many ill-assorted subjects and great social changes were ripping apart the old fabric. Subject nations wanted their independence. The 1848 revolution had made the Emperor Franz Joseph determined to resist all change but it was like trying to hold on the lid of a pressure cooker by manual force.

Franz Joseph was a rigid disciplinarian, who rose at 4 a.m. to work on state papers; his life was one of exact routine. His empress, Elizabeth, was beautiful and sensitive and she found the atmosphere of her husband's court − dominated by her mother-in-law − impossible to stomach; she spent most of her time travelling over Europe, permanently dissatisfied.

Her eldest son Rudolf had his father's obstinacy and his mother's sensitiveness. Born in August 1858, he became an army officer and took pride in the number of his sexual conquests, entering their names in a ledger − red for aristocrats, black for commoners. He grew bored with seduction and flirted with left-wing ideas. Later, he wrote newspaper articles that revealed he had considerable literary talent. He was indeed highly intelligent.

It seems conceivable that at some point he contracted venereal disease. What is certain is that he contracted the rich dilettante's disease of boredom and a sense of meaninglessness. 'He seemed to doubt the validity of everything he did', says one commentator: His father declined to allow him any taste of responsibility. At twenty-three he was married to the seventeen-year-old Princess Stephanie of Belgium, a silly, selfish, empty-headed girl, who bore him a daughter. Rudolf became increasingly depressed and listless, and began to take morphine. When the German emperor inspected Franz Joseph's army in 1888, he protested that the infantry ought not to be in the charge of an incompetent like Rudolf; he was removed — one more blow to his self-esteem. To some brother officers he made the surprising proposal of a suicide pact, which they failed to take seriously, although it was reported to the police.

His relationship with his father became increasingly bitter. He began to plot, in a rather half-hearted manner, his father's downfall. His friend Count Stephen Károlyi was a Hungarian patriot and he planned to speak in the Hungarian parliament against granting funds to Franz Joseph's army. Rudolf seems to have agreed to a harebrained scheme of Károlyi's to oust Franz Joseph and put him on the throne. (It might, in fact, have saved the Austrian empire if it had ever happened, since Rudolf's liberal tendencies may have defused the tensions.) A butler reported that the emperor bitterly upbraided his son for disloyalty.

Maria Vetsera was an attractive teenager of Greek extraction, whose mother had married into the minor Austrian nobility. She caught a few glimpses of Rudolf in society and decided she was passionately in love with him. Through her friend, Countess Marie Larisch, who was Rudolf's cousin, she succeeded in being presented to him in the Prater in Vienna. Rudolf was not one to turn down the opportunity to accept a girl's virginity when it was

Archduke Rudolf of Habsburg

offered; the two became lovers in 1888. By this time he was
already brooding on suicide.

On 28 January 1889, Rudolf received a telegram from
Budapest. As he threw it aside he was heard to mutter, 'It
has to be. There is no other way.' He spent the day writing
farewell letters, then set out for his hunting lodge at
Mayerling. He had arranged to meet Maria on the way;
that morning, she slipped away from her mother and made
off in a carriage sent by Rudolf. It seems likely that she had
already agreed to the suicide pact. They met at an inn.

Rudolf had arranged a hunting party at his lodge and
various friends were also there. But on 29 January, 1889, he
protested that he had a cold and stayed indoors. That
evening, he dined with Count Hoyos, while Maria stayed
upstairs. When Hoyos left, Rudolf's valet, Loschek, entertained them by singing for them. They both wrote farewell
letters – Maria told her sister: 'We are both going blissfully
into the uncertain beyond . . .' They then discussed
whether they preferred to die by poison or a bullet and
decided on the revolver. Maria noted this decision on an
ashtray. They went up to the bedroom where Rudolf shot
Maria immediately. He himself waited until six in the
morning, when he went downstairs and told Loschek to
prepare breakfast. He returned to his room, drank a glass of
brandy, and shot himself in the head. The bodies were
discovered a few hours later.

Franz Joseph was deeply shocked by the news, and the
empress broke down when she read Rudolf's farewell letter.
At first the court insisted that Rudolf had died of heart
failure but the truth could not be held back for ever. There
was a wrangle with the Cardinal Secretary of State,
Rampolla, as to whether Rudolf could be buried in con-
secrated ground as he had committed suicide. Eventually he
was laid to rest in the Capucin Crypt in Vienna. Maria's
naked body was thrown into a woodshed immediately after
she was discovered and was not recovered for two days.

Queen Boudicca of Britain – better known as
Boadicea – fought a war against the occupying
Romans around 61 AD. Her brutality was
legendary. Here is a description by a Roman
historian, Dio Cassius, of London after Boudicca
had plundered it:

'Those who were taken captive by the Britons
were subjected to every known outrage . . .
they hung up the noblest and most distinguished
women and they cut off their breasts and sewed
them to their mouths in order to make the
victims appear to be eating them; afterwards
they impaled the women on sharp skewers run
lengthwise through the entire body. All this
they did to the accompaniment of sacrifices,
banquets and wanton behaviour.

It is still not clear why Rudolf killed himself and why he,
a Catholic, chose to die with the murder of Maria Vetsera
on his conscience. The answer to the latter question may be
that he was a physical coward and wanted someone else to
die with him. He was probably not in love with Maria for he
had spent the night before leaving Vienna with a prostitute
named Mizzi Kaspter. It seems conceivable that she was as
anxious to die with the man she adored as he was to have
someone to die with him. He may even have felt he was
conferring a favour on her by involving her in the suicide
pact – after all, he was heir to the throne and she was a
nobody.

In 1983, ex-Empress Zita, the last survivor of the
Habsburg monarchy, caused a sensation when she announced that the double-suicide was really a political
murder. She claimed that she had received this information

from her husband, Emperor Karl, and from Prince Rudolf's sisters, Archduchess Gisela and Archduchess Marie-Valerie and her aunts Archduchess Maria Theresia and the Duchess Marie-José. 'I have recorded precisely everything that was told to me under the seal of deepest sympathy. I intend to publish these documents which are among my personal papers when the time is right.' According to the ex-Empress, Prince Rudolf was assassinated because of his republican sympathies and because he had made many political enemies. In a cloister built out of part of the hunting lodge, Carmelite nuns in a silent order still pray day and night for the 'three dead' of Mayerling. Why three, rather than two, remains another mystery; according to some, Maria Vetsera was expecting Rudolf's child.

The Empress points out that an enormous amount of documentation has disappeared from the state archives, including a 2,000-word telegram which the Emperor sent to Pope Leo XIII arguing that in spite of the official suicide explanation, his son had a right to a Christian burial. This telegram has also disappeared from the Vatican archives.

In September 1898, the Empress Elizabeth was stepping into a boat at Geneva when she was stabbed to death by a young anarchist named Luigi Lucheni. There were those who felt her death was a release. Since Rudolf's suicide she had been wandering all over Europe like an unhappy shade.

Rudolf was succeeded as heir to the throne by his cousin, Archduke Franz Ferdinand. It was the assassination of the archduke and his wife at Sarajevo on 28 June 1914 that precipitated World War I, and brought about the final destruction of the Austrian Empire.

Maria Vetsera, mistress of Archduke Rudolf

Chapter Six

QUEEN VICTORIA AND JOHN BROWN

S candal involving the widowed Queen Victoria and her Court favourite, ghillie John Brown, reached such proportions in the 1860s that there were genuine fears for the future of the monarchy in Britain. Republicanism had already swept Europe in 1848, the year of the Communist manifesto of Marx and Engels. Now it was on the rise in Britain, feeding off poverty and the struggle for electoral reform. Disenchantment with the monarchy stemmed from the Queen's virtual disappearance from public life following the death of the Prince Consort in 1861. Now rumours of her 'affair' with John Brown, the one-time stable lad who had been appointed Victoria's Personal Highland Servant – with explicit instructions to take orders from no one but herself – fell on doubly fertile ground, both within the Establishment and with the mob.

That Queen Victoria and John Brown loved each other is a matter of record. After Brown's death in 1883, she wrote to his brother Hugh: 'So often I told him that no one loved him more than I did or had a better friend than me . . . and he answered, "Nor you than me. No one loves you more."' What has always remained the subject for speculation, and scandal, is if that love was strictly platonic. When rumour was at its height the Press sailed as close to the wind as it dared, pillorying Brown personally and the Queen by inference, in savagely slanted reports and cartoons. One Swiss newspaper, the *Gazette de Lausanne*, 'reported' their secret marriage, adding for good measure that Victoria was pregnant by Brown. An American diarist visiting Britain in 1868 wrote in *Tinsley's Magazine*: 'Soon after my arrival in London at a table where all the company were gentlemen by rank or position, there were constant references to and jokes about "Mrs Brown" . . . I lost the point of all the witty sayings and should have remained in blissful ignorance throughout the dinner, had not my host kindly informed me that "Mrs Brown" was an English synonym for the Queen . . .' And if, after all that and much more, there were those left who still harboured any doubts about the relationship between the Queen and John Brown, their doubts must surely have been dispelled after her death in 1901, when her eldest son, now King Edward VII, ordered all his mother's treasured photographs of John Brown to be burned, his busts destroyed, and − pettiest of all − the ghillie's apartment at Windsor Castle, undisturbed since his death, to be turned into a billiards room.

John Brown, second of a family of eleven children, was born at Crathienaird, opposite Balmoral on the north bank of the Dee, on 8 December 1826. His father was the local schoolmaster, his mother a blacksmith's daughter. He started working life as ostler's boy at a coaching inn, joined the staff on Balmoral estate (then rented by a Scottish knight) as a 13-shillings-a-week stable hand and was retained as an under-groom when it passed into royal ownership in 1848. His rise in royal favour was swift. By 1858 'Johnny Brown' had been specially appointed to attend on the Queen, doubling as 'keeper' to Prince Albert. When the Queen and her husband began their 'Great Expeditions' in the Highlands in 1860, travelling incognito from Balmoral to stay at country inns and shooting lodges, Brown accompanied them as Victoria's valet. She wrote gushingly of him to her uncle, King Leopold I of the Belgians: 'He takes wonderful care of me, combining the offices of groom, footman, page and maid, I might almost say, as he is so handy about cloaks and shawls.'

Queen Victoria and John Brown

Queen Victoria, the British queen whose name is synonymous with staid sexual attitudes and exaggerated propriety, may have been illegitimate. The theory is put forward in the book *Queen Victoria's Gene* by D.M. Potts and W.T.W. Potts.

Their theory rests upon the fact that some of Queen Victoria's offspring carried the gene for haemophilia, an inherited disease that prevents the blood from clotting. The disorder only affects male offspring; female children with the gene pass it on to their children without being affected.

It is known from the meticulous records of European royal houses that Edward, Duke of Kent, Victoria's supposed father, was not a sufferer. Records relating to Princess Victoire, Victoria's mother, do not exist. However, by the time that she married the Duke of Kent, Victoire had already married once, and produced two children. If she were a carrier, one would expect haemophilia to show up in these two children, or in their descendants. Records show that that branch of the royal family tree was free from the disease. It is is therefore very unlikely that Victoria had inherited the disease.

So where did the gene come from? It could have been a fresh mutation in Victoria or her mother. In other words, the disease could have started spontaneously in either of the two women. As only 1 in 100,000 people per generation develop the haemophilia mutation,

this is unlikely. This leaves the possibility that
the Duke of Kent was not Victoria's father.

The authors of *Queen Victoria's Gene* suggest that
Victoire could have chosen a lover to father her
child because her husband Edward was infertile.
Evidence for this, they say, can be found in the
fact that Edward's mistress, with whom he slept
for many years, never got pregnant. This was
very uncommon in the early nineteenth century.
William IV's mistress, for example, had ten
children over the course of their affair.

But why would Victoire cuckold her husband?
At the time of Victoria's birth no child of
George III had managed to have a legitimate,
living child. George IV himself had no heirs. His
brother William, who succeeded him, was
beginning to look to old to produce a successor.
And so it proved.

It seems possible that the phrase 'Victorian
values' may have to be redefined.

Victoria's mother, the Duchess of Kent, died in March
1861 and her husband Albert, of typhoid fever in December
the same year. At forty-two she found herself in that
unique, gilded-cage isolation known only to Monarchy,
as mother of nine children as well as Queen of the world's
greatest power. Perhaps not surprisingly she became so
overwhelmed by grief and responsibility that many considered her behaviour unbalanced, even a little mad.
Henceforth a photograph of her dead spouse was to hang
a foot above every bed she slept in, with a plaster cast of his
hand on the dressing table nearby. The royal servants laid
out a clean nightshirt each night for his ghost and as
solemnly brought in hot shaving water every morning.

Albert's rooms at Buckingham Palace, Windsor, Osborne and Balmoral were sealed and their contents photographed, so that after cleaning each article could be restored to the exact spot it occupied at the moment of his death. So overwrought did she become that she blamed her son Bertie, the Prince of Wales (and a notorious rake) for hastening his father's death by his affairs. Tearful and brooding, she went into a *purdah* of mourning for several years, wilfully neglecting her royal duties to the point of forfeiting public sympathy and even loyalty.

It was into this unreal world of permanent mourning and near madness that John Brown was summoned in December 1864. He arrived at Osborne, the Queen's home on the Isle of Wight, in kilt and bonnet and leading her favourite pony through the snow, harnessed to her own carriage brought from Balmoral. As medicine, it worked from the start. According to author E.E.P. Tisdall: 'It was said that the smile which lit the Queen's face was the first which had been seen since that dreadful night.' Unfortunately while Brown's presence signalled the start of the Queen's return to normality, it also gave rise to gossip. She was still only forty-five and a passionate woman. Brown was thirty-eight, a handsome, red-headed giant of a man, already devoted to her. If it was only natural that she should rely more and more on this one man who was never far from her side, it was perhaps also inevitable that tongues should soon start to wag; especially as Brown had a positive genius for upsetting all but Her Majesty with his gruff, no-nonsense manner.

Within two months of his arrival at Osborne he had been appointed the Queen's 'Personal Highland Servant', at a salary of £120 a year, with instructions to attend her both indoors and out and to take his orders 'from none but herself'. This he interpreted literally and while his respect for his royal mistress was sincere, no one could ever accuse him of kow-towing to her. He addressed her as an equal, calling her 'wumman', openly scolding her for taking insufficient care with her appearance. ('What are ye daein' wi' that auld dress on ye agen?') No one else in Britain would have dared to speak to her in such a way and when extended to senior members of the Household it caused the deepest resentment. General Sir Charles Grey, her Personal Secretary, bristled at Brown's offhand manner when bearing royal messages. A clash with equerry General Sir John M'Neil brought a fiery retort from Brown, 'Dinna be abrupt wi' me, I'm nae one of ye're private sodgers' and, within hours, an implied rebuke from the Queen, offering the General a remote command in India should he choose to accept it. Ministers-in-waiting knew better than to offend this former ghillie who wielded such immense influence with the Queen but few loved him for that.

The Queen's first, reluctant efforts to regain goodwill by appearing in public served only to worsen the situation. In February 1866, she opened Parliament for the first time since Albert's death in 1861 but disappointed the crowds by eschewing all pomp and pageantry, even entering the Palace of Westminster by a side door. The following month she reviewed a parade of troops at Aldershot, likewise for the first time in years; but instead of sitting on her own horse to take the salute, as of yore, she remained in her carriage – leaving John Brown in full view, on the box above.

Rumours of the 'association' were already rife; now they multiplied, with Brown the target for attack. In June, rumour said, 'Brown was to blame' for the Queen's failure to return immediately to London from Balmoral, following the defeat of Lord John Russell's government. In July, their mutual fondness for whisky ('Begg's Best', distilled on the Balmoral estate, was a favourite tipple) was used as a weapon by the reporters keeping watch on the royal holiday there. According to rumour, John Brown had been mortally offended by a mock Court Circular in *Punch* which debunked him, so much so that he tendered his resignation in drunken fury when the Queen dared to laugh at the article. Soon the *John O' Groats Journal* published a letter from its London correspondent:

> I suppose all my readers have heard of the great Court favourite John Brown. His dismissal some weeks ago was generally talked about at the time, and I observe that the fact has now found its way into print, coupled with the suggestion of John Brown's probable restoration to power before long. The reason assigned for his dismissal is an inordinate indulgence in the national taste for whisky, and the restraining of that appetite is mentioned as a likely condition of his readmission to favour. Far be it from me to question Mr Brown's powers of suction. They may rival those of Dickens' character, the elder Weller, I think, who would have made an uncommon good oyster if he'd been born in that sphere of life . . . But Brown's fall has been more commonly ascribed to *Mr Punch* than to any shortcomings of his own . . .

In September 1866 an anonymous 'Special Correspondent' of the *Gazette de Lausanne* said in print what the rumour-mongers in London society were saying at their dinner tables – that the Queen had secretly married Brown in a morganatic ceremony, and was avoiding public appearances to try to hide the fact that she was pregnant again. 'They say that with Brown and by him she consoles herself for Prince Albert, and they go even further. They add that she is in an interesting condition, and that if she was not present for the Volunteers Review, and at the inauguration of the monument to Prince Albert, it was only in order to hide her pregnancy. I hasten to add that the Queen has been morganatically married to her attendant for a long time, which diminishes the gravity of the thing . . .'

Queen Victoria

Queen Victoria and John Brown

In his book *Queen Victoria's Private Life* author E.E.P. Tisdall (who discounted the notion that the affair was platonic) says that a pamphlet entitled *Mrs John Brown* was privately printed in Britain '. . . to circulate very widely in stately homes and servants' halls . . . The pamphlet declared that the Queen had married John Brown at a secret ceremony. It was never discovered who had paid for the printing and organized the distribution of the pamphlet, but a suggestion was made that the money came from the funds of the Republican party, which was active and growing, as might be expected with such a queer state of affairs existing around the Throne . . .'

To boost circulation, the satirical magazine *Tomahawk* lost no time in joining the anti-royalist pack. In its first issue of May 1867, the caption to a caricature of Landseer's painting of Victoria on horseback at Osborne, attended by John Brown, read slyly: 'All is black that is not Brown.' In his painting, the artist had over-emphasized the Queen in mourning; not only did he show her in full widow's weeds, mounted on a black charger, he even put Brown into a black kilt. The public, who flocked to the Royal Academy's Spring Exhibition — and had heard all the rumours — first giggled and finally laughed out loud on seeing the painting. Press comment was brutal. Said the *Saturday Review*: 'We respect the privacy of Her Majesty but when Sir Edwin Landseer puts the Queen and her black favourites into what are, during the season, the most public rooms in England, he does more harm to her popularity than he imagines.'

Tomahawk's June edition carried a more spiteful cartoon. This time it portrayed an empty Throne, with the royal robes flung across it and alongside, an equally neglected Crown — under a glass dust-cover. The caption asked bluntly: 'Where is Britannia?' The magazine's August cartoon was downright vicious. Captioned: 'A Brown Study', it showed kilted John Brown leaning indolently on the vacant Throne, with a clay pipe in his hand, wearing a bonnet and hobnailed ghillie's boots, staring down unconcernedly at an angry British Lion. Tisdall called it '. . . the most daring and ferocious anti-royalist cartoon ever seen in Britain, or possibly anywhere, in a public journal . . . If such an insult to the Sovereign appeared today in the Press, questions in Parliament and assurances from the Prime Minister would doubtless be followed by a sensational prosecution. But nothing followed the publication of "A Brown Study" . . . except an uproar of bitter laughter . . . Nobody called attention to it in the House; Ministers of the Crown kept their silence. They suspected that *Tomahawk* with its "Brown Study" was more or less telling the truth.'

By July 1867, government fears of a hostile demonstration against the Queen were such that an excuse was invented to cancel a military review in Hyde Park rather than risk her attendance there in the company of John Brown. Although she had agreed, reluctantly, to the Prime Minister's suggestion to leave Brown at home to avoid possible incidents 'of an unpleasant nature', the Cabinet feared she might defy ministerial advice and take Brown anyway. So, the assassination in far-off Mexico of the Emperor Maximilian (a distant relative, by marriage, of the Queen) was used as a pretext to put the Court back into mourning and cancel the review altogether.

The year 1871 saw the Republican movement reach its zenith in Britain and not only because of her supposed dalliance with Brown. In an age when 15 *s.* a week was a factory hand's wage, a request that Parliament should approve a dowry of £30,000, plus an annuity, on the Queen's daughter, Princess Louise's marriage to the Marquis of Lorne, dismayed even the most ardent royalist supporters. The Queen herself was even accused in a pamphlet of misappropriating public funds. Signed by a critic styling himself 'Solomon Temple', and headed 'What Does She Do With It?', the pamphlet complained that cash saved from Civil List funds was diverted to her own account.

Neglect of royal duties was still the main weapon in the Republican armoury, however. *The Times* labelled Queen Victoria 'The Great Absentee', while to the *Pall Mall Gazette* she had become 'The Invisible Monarch'. When she fell ill in the autumn of that year no medical bulletins were issued, so that the country remained unaware of her condition even though, at one stage, she was apparently not expected to live another twenty-four hours. In contrast, when the Prince of Wales (himself no stranger to scandal) went down that winter with typhoid fever — the same illness which had killed his father ten years earlier — the whole nation prayed for his recovery. This time bulletins were issued and as the Prince's condition reached crisis point, so the public attitude to the Royal Family changed to one of compassion and sympathy. ('An epidemic . . . of typhoid loyalty', sneered the anti-royalist *Reynold's News*.) So complete was the turn-around, however, that by mid-December 1871, when the royal recovery was assured, republicanism in Britain was a spent force.

In 1889, while a guest of Queen Victoria, the Shah of Persia attempted to buy the Marchioness of Londonderry. On another occasion the Shah was under the impression that all the female guests at a particular social event were the Prince of Wales' wives. Unimpressed by the Prince's 'harem' he suggested that they all be beheaded and some more attractive women found.

Now it was Brown's turn to benefit from the wind of change. On 27 February 1872 a Thanksgiving Service for the Prince's recovery was held at St Paul's Cathedral. Two days later the Queen drove through Regent's Park in an open carriage, accompanied by her sons Alfred and Leopold, to thank her subjects for their demonstration of loyalty. Brown was on the box, as always. As the carriage re-entered Buckingham Palace a young man scaled the railings, ran up and pointed a pistol at the Queen's face. In the split-second of confusion which followed the two Princes hesitated, as did the mounted equerries nearby. Brown alone proved equal to the occasion. As the Queen screamed, 'Save me!' and flung herself against her Lady-in-Waiting, Lady Jane Churchill, he leapt down and shouldered the gunman aside, then pursued him as he made for the other side of the carriage. He described what happened next to Bow Street magistrates, 'I took hold o' him wi' one o' my hauns, and I grippit him wi' the other by the scruff o' the neck . . . till half a dizzen had a grip o' him, grooms, equerries, I kenna' how mony there was . . .'

The pistol was later found to be defective, the intruder mentally unstable, but none of that detracted from John Brown's courage or presence of mind. In the eyes of the public, at least, he was transformed at a stroke from villain to hero. The Queen presented him with a new award, the Devoted Service Medal, which carried with it an annuity of £25 (but lapsed with his death; John Brown was the sole recipient). She later made him 'John Brown, Esquire' and he was listed in *Whitaker's Almanack* as a member of the Household, at a salary of £400 a year.

After his death (from erysipelas) in 1883, aged only fifty-six, he lay in state for six days, in the Clarence Tower at Windsor. His Court Circular obituary occupied twenty-five lines, compared with Disraeli's five lines, two years earlier. The Queen attended his funeral service at Windsor, although most of her family found excuses to be elsewhere. Her card on his coffin read: 'A tribute of loving, grateful, and ever-lasting friendship and affection from his truest, best, and most faithful friend, Victoria. R & I.' Five hundred mourners attended his burial at Crathie, on 5 April 1883. His opponents within the Establishment were to have the last word, however. Encouraged by the success of her previous book, *More Leaves from the Journal of a Life in the Highlands*, which she had dedicated to Brown, the Queen now declared her intention of writing *The Life of Brown*. Her Household was appalled, knowing it could only revive the scandal, but lacked the courage to say so. It was left to the Dean of Windsor (The Reverend Randall Davidson, later Archbishop of Canterbury) to urge her, after reading the rough draft, not to publish. When she persisted, he offered to resign — and the Queen gave in.

After his mother's death in 1901, Edward VII inflicted the final indignities on Brown's memory, as mentioned above, by ordering her photographs of him to be burned, and his quarters at Windsor turned into a games room. Author Tom Cullen wrote a fitting epitaph for the best-loved and most hated of all British royal servants in his book *The Empress Brown*: 'Although John Brown has been dead for eighty-six years, his bones still rattle in the Royal closet at Windsor, where, as a subject for scandal he is regarded as second to the Abdication . . .'

Chapter Seven

LUDWIG AND LOLA

When Ludwig I of Bavaria came to the throne in 1825, the country was peaceful and prosperous. His father Maximilian had read the situation astutely during the wars with Napoleon, supporting him until it became unwise, then switching sides in time to join the rest of Europe's victory celebrations. As a result Bavaria had been left relatively unravaged by the war that had devastated most of Europe.

The von Kaulbach portrait of Ludwig reveals that he was handsome in a smooth-skinned Germanic way, but his expression suggests a craving for admiration rather than the respect due to a king. His moustache is jaunty but surprisingly small for a European monarch of the time – the fashion being for the mouth-obscuring walrus variety, often accompanied by a beard of equal proportions. His rejection of the martial image of his predecessors can be traced to the fact that he was deafened as a child by the blast of a cannon.

Like his hero Lord Byron, Ludwig (or Louis) was enchanted by the ruins and monuments of the ancient world. To his eye Bavaria, though full of natural beauty, somehow lacked the decaying grandeur of Greece or Rome. To remedy this, archaeologists were despatched regularly to bring back as much picturesque decay and as they could lay their hands on. Throughout Bavaria Ludwig raised vast monuments to the arts of past and present times. He turned Munich into one of the great cultural centres of Europe. At Ratisbon, where a replica of the Parthenon was built, he erected a statue of himself in a Roman toga. He was also a generous patron of the arts – at least, of those that he did not practise himself. The poet Heinrich Heine was banished from Bavaria: Ludwig wrote his own poetry.

Not everyone was happy to see an art lover on the throne. His Austrian neighbour Prince Metternich — a rigid conservative — viewed it all with deep distrust. In his youth Ludwig had had a reputation as a leftist, and even though he later became a reactionary, his attempt to turn Bavaria into 'the Athens of Germany' struck Metternicht as a sign of feeble-mindedness. Fortunately, Ludwig still had a sentimental regard for the Church, so Metternicht sent in the Jesuits, then watched with satisfaction as they gained political control. In the rest of Europe they were already a spent force, but in Bavaria they found a comfortable refuge, running the country while the king wrote poetry and wandered around art galleries.

As a result of all this, the liberal Bavarian constitution of 1818, a document that Ludwig himself had helped to draft, was generally ignored. Despite the protestations of his parliament, the Diet, Ludwig allowed the Jesuits to do their best to restore the Middle Ages.

So twenty years drifted by like a peaceful summer afternoon, during which time Bavaria became a kind of time capsule, an oasis of nostalgia for the Middle Ages. It was highly popular with tourists.

Then the storm arrived.

One day in 1846, Ludwig was sitting at his desk, arranging the affairs of state, when he was disturbed by a struggle in the corridor. Before he had had time to ask his aide what was going on, the office door flew open and a woman burst in, wrestling vigorously with two members of the Royal guard. She was dressed in the costume of a Spanish dancer, the dress slightly torn from the melee.

What followed was obviously designed to prevent the king from having her thrown out. Pulling a knife from her bosom, the mysterious woman slit the front of her dress open from breast to hem, whereupon it fell to the floor.

The king cleared his throat and, adjusting his pince nez, asked the guards and the aide to leave. Then he asked the half-naked stranger what she wanted. When she began to speak, he explained he was deaf, and that she would have to come closer. Accordingly, she bent over and placed her mouth against his ear. At close quarters it became apparent that she had stunning blue eyes.

This was Lola Montez, adventuress, mistress of men of genius, and dancer of questionable talent. Her origins were unknown, the subject of much gossip and speculation. She was said to be the daughter of a famous matador — or, according to her own preferred version, an illegitimate daughter of European royalty. Even her original nationality was a mystery; she could speak nine languages, including Hindustani, all of them with a foreign accent. By the time of her unceremonious introduction to Ludwig, she was known in the capitals of Europe as an ambitious woman who lived on her sex appeal — a kind of 19th century Holly Golightly.

According to her memoirs, she had not only taken part in the Warsaw uprising of 1830, but caused it. Poland at that time was occupied by the Russians. The Russian viceroy conceived a violent passion for Lola, and tried to seduce her with promises of power, jewellery and money. She turned them down on the grounds that he was ugly and a oppressor of the Polish people. The incensed viceroy engaged henchmen to boo Miss Montez on the Warsaw stage, where she danced nightly before her ecstatic public. Finally tiring of these noisy interlopers, she approached the footlights and denounced them to the rest of the audience, telling them that they had been hired by the viceroy and were under the protection of theatre's director, a Russian sympathizer. The patriotic Poles browbeat the hecklers into silence, and later formed a mass escort to protect Lola on her way back to her hotel. After this, according to Lola, they revolted against the Russian garrison and expelled them from Polish soil. In the subsequent chaos, Lola herself was saved by a gallant French consul who spirited her out of the country before the police could take their revenge.

The only part of this story it is possible to verify is that she was in Warsaw at the time of the uprising. It is also possible that she was booed while onstage, although not necessarily for the reasons that she gives.

This 'dangerous and beautiful tigress' – as she once described herself – first came to the attention of the gossip columnists (who were just as numerous then as they are now) as the mistress of Franz Liszt. The composer, whose own sex appeal often caused female admirers to faint during his piano recitals, found her intoxicating, and for a while they were seen everywhere together. Liszt decided to end the liaison when Lola was inspired to dance on the table at a dinner at which Queen Victoria (q.v.) and Prince Albert were present. Liszt abandoned her in the dead of night, taking the precaution of paying the landlord for the furniture he knew she would devastate in the morning.

After this, she became a familiar figure in the salons of most European capitals, specialising in exercising her charm on famous men – after Liszt, she became the mistress of Alexandre Dumas. One of her few notable failures was with Richard Wagner, who described her as 'a painted woman with insolent eyes' – but then, Wagner preferred docile women. The peak of her notoriety came when one of her lovers, a journalist named Dujarier, fought a duel over her and was killed. At the murder trial, subduing her sobs, she told the court that she should have fought the duel in the place her lover, for she was a far better shot.

After this bereavement, she returned to dancing and it was in 1846, when she was in her late twenties, that she brought herself so compellingly to the attention of King Ludwig.

She had come to see the king to complain about the manager of the Munich theatre in which she was booked to perform. The manager had broken his contract on the

Hungarian pianist and composer, Franz Liszt

grounds that her dancing was atrocious. In a rage Lola had made her way to the royal palace to ask what kind of a philistine country this was.

What passed when the two were left alone can only be surmised, although there can be no doubt that the romantic Ludwig, whose role model was Lord Byron, was as susceptible as the next man to a half naked lady with a superb figure. We only know that, five days later, when he summoned his ministers, his Jesuits advisers and his court to meet the woman he described as 'his best friend', it was plain to all that the old and deaf king was in a trance of admiration. The Jesuits were particularly unhappy, since Lola obviously reminded the king of his Byronic youth, and the distant days when he regarded himself as a Liberal — she could only upset the stability they had fought so hard to establish.

Dismay grew as they became aware of the extent of Ludwig's infatuation. He announced that she was to star in a solo royal command performance, a fitting retort to her Munich theatre manager. The invited, not to say compelled, audience did their best to show that they appreciated her talents, and the king and Lola were ecstatic. Fortunately there were no professional critics present to say what they really thought.

No one was worried about the moral aspect of taking a mistress — least of all the Jesuits; what Ludwig did on his office divan was his own affair. What worried them was Lola's political opinions. Mixing with the liberal intelligentsia during her travels around Europe, she had inevitably picked up some progressive ideas. Now she saw herself as mistress of a poet-king whose ministers and advisers were all boring reaction-aries. She could see that it was not her lover's fault — he was simply that he had always been more interested in art than in politics. Now she was prepared to undertake his political education.

One morning at the breakfast table, Ludwig began to
read her his latest poem, which began:

> By thee my life becomes ennobled,
> Which without thee was solitary and empty
> Thy love is the nutriment of my heart;
> If it had it not, it would die!

At this juncture, Lola interrupted him to point out that if
he really wanted to ennoble his life, he should start by
breaking the stranglehold of the Jesuits on his country.
After all, the administration was mainly Jesuit, the Prime
Minister Baron Abel was a Jesuit, and the schools and
universities were run by Jesuits.

The king was inclined to agree, but pointed out that
there were too many of them to get rid of — the whole
administration would collapse.

Then why not, said Lola, start at the top and work down?
Begin by sacking Baron Abel.

Ludwig pondered the matter, and decided that he had
never really liked Baron Abel — certainly not as much as he
liked Lola. There were also a few things about the Jesuits
that irritated him. Why not take her advice? Ludwig began
to calculate how he could gently dislodge his Prime
Minister.

Understandably, the Jesuits dug in their heels, and did
their best to remind the king that he was the ruler of a
Catholic country, and had a duty to his people. But their
own teachings militated against them. They had encouraged Ludwig to feel that he was the absolute ruler of the
country, and to ignore liberal nonsense about democracy.
Now Ludwig ignored them. The Jesuit press made things
worse by declaring that Lola was the whore from Revelation, and since Ludwig knew she was nothing of the sort,
this had the effect of hardening his heart. Finally, when the
cabinet opposed his decision to make Lola a Bavarian

citizen, he got rid them, and appointed a liberal cabinet headed by Graf Zu Rhein, which had no objection to Lola being made Countess Landsberg, as well as Baroness Rosenthal.

Outside Bavaria word of the king's folly was spreading. In desperation Ludwig's sister, Archduchess Sophie of Austria, wrote to him begging that he abandon this loathsome little gold-digger. Ludwig did not reply.

Julius Caesar, first emperor of Rome, was dogged for most of his career by the rumour that he had been the lover of King Nicomedes of Bithynia. The scandal would not die down and is recorded in many cutting descriptions.
Licinius Calvus published the lines: 'The riches of Bithynia's King / Who Caesar on his couch abused.' Curio the Elder called him: 'Nicomedes' Bithynian brothel.' It was Bibulus, Caesar's co-consul, who put it most succinctly: 'The Queen of Bithynia . . . who once wanted to sleep with a monarch, but now wants to be one.'

The new cabinet reflected Lola's desires and opinions so exactly that it became known as the Lolaministerium. And Ludwig demonstrated the extent of his devotion to Lola when he diverted a stream of funding for the arts to build her a fairy-tale palace furnished with a glass staircase and paintings pirated from the public galleries. But when Lola asked for a private chapel and a confessor, Ludwig had to explain with embarrassment that there was not a single priest in the country who would accept the job.

The sudden ascent to power and wealth had an adverse effect on Lola's temperament. Here temper, which had always been volatile, grew worse. She slapped the face of the chief of police, threw a priceless vase at the head of her interior decorator, and kicked a champagne bucket, complete with bottle and ice, across the room. One student wrote: 'I am the only friend she ever had at whom she never threw a plate or a book, or attacked with a dagger, poker, broom or other deadly weapon.'

The liberals were delighted with her. So were the Protestants. So were other nations who had their reservations about Bavaria and its Jesuits, including England. Yet the Bavarian people themselves were unhappy. Freedom of the press was all very well, but it was a pity that they owed it to a woman who was admitted to having had dozens of lovers, and was therefore not the kind of person that any decent citizen could admire. Besides, the free press used its freedom to publish cartoons of Lola that bordered on the obscene. Even in the Protestant north of the country, she was booed.

The university students, a group which in modern times can always be relied upon for liberal rhetoric, were in Lola's Bavaria implacably opposed to her reforms — for they accepted the word of their Jesuit professors that she was ruining the country. But not all students were against her: a band of twenty acted as her bodyguard, and lived in a house in the palace grounds. The group was known as 'The Alemannia', and her housekeeper later claimed that Lola had long and energetic orgies with them, a rumour that seems to have been common at the time. Professor Johann Dollinger, a Catholic divine wrote to a friend: 'For Lola Montez they formed a sort of male harem, and the particulars which have transpired, and with which, of course, I must not pollute your ears, leave no doubt that she is a second Messalina.' Messalina, students of Roman history will recall, once had an orgy with a cohort of Roman soldiers and left them all in a state of collapse.

Royal Scandals

For two years Lola was the de facto ruler of Bavaria, in spite of attempts by the Jesuits, conservative politicians and concerned neighbours like Metternich. She was a combination of irresistable force and immovable object. Ludwig would simply sack anyone who criticized her.

Inevitably, outraged citizens — particularly women — took every opportunity to snub her; when she went to the theatre they quietly vacated the surrounding boxes, and when she walked through the market, even peasant women drew aside their skirts as if she was covered in mud. No one enjoys being the object of hatred, and Lola began to show mild symptoms of paranoia — for example, she bought herself a bulldog and trained it to attack Jesuits.

It was the dog that indirectly caused Lola's downfall. One day when out walking, she encountered a Professor von Lassaulx, a teacher of philosophy at the university, and his hostile expression was enough to make her set her dog on him. Von Lassaulx called a meeting of fellow professors to protest, and the king reacted by sacking them all. This in turn provoked the students to riot on behalf of their tutors. They gathered outside Lola's palace and threw stones. Lola's reaction was to taunt them by standing on her balcony drinking champagne and tossing them expensive chocolates, as well as her bulldog, which did its best to bite as many ankles as possible. She had reason to be confident: a cordon of soldiers prevented the students from smashing down the door and destroying the house.

Finally, Ludwig's coach appeared, and a silence fell on the crowd. Without appearing to notice the rioters, Ludwig went inside. When he left a few hours later, the remnants that remained shouted insults — the first time in his life the king had been publicly defied.

For three days the capital looked like a war-zone; the students erected barriers against the army, and Lola's windows had to be covered with wire mesh. She was a prisoner in her own house. Yet she remained unrepentant.

When mobs booed her, she harangued them about freedom, and they were reluctantly forced to admit that she had courage. Ludwig certainly thought so; he regarded her as the perfect mate for a philosopher-king, and ignored all criticism. Eventually, things returned to an uneasy normality. That was in 1847.

Then 1848 arrived – the year of revolution throughout Europe: in Berlin, Vienna, Venice, Rome, Milan, Naples, Prague and Budapest. In Paris, King Louis Philippe tried to ban a 'political banquet' of liberals, and when soldiers fired into the crowd, had a revolution on his hands – the king had to flee to England. And in Munich, Ludwig made the mistake of trying to suppress student unrest by closing the university. It was the worst thing he could have done. The students took to the streets and erected barricades. Lola's Alemmania were attacked by right wing students in a cafe, and when Lola – with typical courage – marched out single-handed to rescue them, she came near to being torn to pieces by the crowd, and had to take refuge – ironically – in a church.

At last, the king saw reason. The mobs surged in the street and his own throne was in danger. Worse still, so was the life of his beloved. Reluctantly, he signed the order for her banishment. A crowd led by a countess and a baroness battered at her gates. Escorted to her coach by her faithful students, Lola finally escaped, pursued by pistol shots and broken bottles.

But she was not beaten yet. Her democratic convictions stopped short at the notion of bowing to the will of the people. She returned to Bavaria disguised as a peasant woman to beg the king to rescind her banishment. Ludwig had her escorted to the Swiss border. She came back dressed as a man; again he sent her away. Recognizing that her tenacity was probably greater than his own, he persuaded her to visit an exorcist, to 'drive the devil out of her'. Perhaps hoping to soften his heart by obedience, she did as he asked. During the enforced imprisonment required by the exorcist, Lola was fed only raspberry juice, and became so thin that her vanity revolted; she was too young to turn into a shrivelled crone. Next time she found the door unlocked, she fled.

Ludwig's cowardice did not save his throne. After so much excitement, everyone wanted a change. Ludwig was forced to give it to them by abdicating in favour of his nephew, who became Maximilian II later the same year.

Lola, calling herself the Countess of Landsfeld, travelled far and wide, trading on her experiences and old connections. Ludwig continued to write to her and send her poems, and his devotion was uninfluenced by the discovery that she had left Bavaria with half the crown jewels. In England, Lola married a wealthy young Guards officer named George Heald, who was a dozen years her junior. His aristocratic relatives were outraged, and hired private investigators to look into her past. They soon discovered that Lola had been married many years earlier to a Captain James in India. Undismayed, Lola explained that her first marriage had been annulled by a special Act of Parliament. When this proved to be untrue, Heald infuriated his relatives by refusing to disown Lola; instead he took her abroad. They lived in Spain, where she proceeded to gamble away her husband's fortune. He remained faithful even when she stabbed him with a dagger; but living with her took its toll, and he is believed to have died of drink.

Returning to the stage when creditors made it a necessity, Lola produced and starred in a dramatization of her time as de facto head of the Bavarian state. *Lola Montez in Bavaria*, her imaginatively-titled play, brought her money and notoriety, the two commodities that Lola loved best. When her popularity as an actress waned, she went to America and arrived in California in time for the Gold Rush. There she married a San Francisco newspaperman, P.P. Hull, settled in Grass Valley, and fascinated the miners with her

Lola Montez, mistress of King Louis I of Bavaria

dancing, particularly the wiggles that made red rubber spiders fall out from under her dress. In her spare time she gave lectures in Europe and the US on how to stay beautiful. For even now, as she approached forty, Lola was still beautiful.

In 1861, at the age of forty-three, she died in America, from the syphilis that Ludwig had given her along with the jewels and the bad poetry. At the time, she was alone and poverty stricken.

Once she was no longer there to cloud the issue, the facts that she had struggled to conceal did not take long to surface.

Her name was Eliza Gilbert and she was Irish. The daughter of an officer in the British East Indian Army and a Dublin milliner, Eliza was born (around 1818) two months after a hasty marriage. The pretensions to Spanish blood were not Lola's invention; her mother christened her Maria Dolores Eliza Roseanna Gilbert. Sent home from India after the death of her father, Lola had enjoyed the life of a respectable middle-class young lady in Ireland. When her mother returned unexpectedly and began shopping with suspicious enthusiasm, Lola guessed correctly that she was to be married to someone in India. Inquiring of the young lieutenant – whose name was James – who had accompanied her mother, Lola discovered that a marriage with an elderly rich officer had been arranged. She lost no time in eloping with the adoring lieutenant. But, according to Lola, he proved unfaithful and she left him. Her mother – who had meanwhile remarried – disowned her, and Lola became a dancer and went on the stage. And within a few years, the name of Lola Montez was notorious in most of the capitals of Europe.

No one is certain how many times she married. Recently though, among the Royal papers of the Wittelsbach family – to which Ludwig belonged – there was discovered a certificate recording the marriage of Miss Lola Montez and

King Ludwig I of Bavaria, dated 1857. This was almost ten years after Lola's tumultuous exit from Bavaria; by 1857, she was thirty-nine and Ludwig seventy-one. It seems, then, that Lola returned to the ex-king nine years after his abdication, and that he was still sufficiently devoted to marry her. No one knows how long she stayed, for the Wittelsbach family seems to have taken some trouble to keep the interlude secret.

In spite of his syphilis, Ludwig outlived her by seven years, dying at the age of eighty in 1868.

Chapter Eight

THE KING AND MRS SIMPSON

No single incident in all that fateful year of 1936, which saw Hitler's troops march into the Rhineland, Mussolini's forces conquer Abyssinia, and the outbreak of civil war in Spain, caused a bigger sensation in the Old World or the New than a love affair between a middle-aged couple, and its aftermath; the love of King Edward VIII for American divorcee Mrs Wallis Simpson. It developed into the greatest of all British royal scandals, since it was seen as a possible threat to the monarchy and thus to the Constitution itself, and it ended in the King's abdication and exile.

The King's love for twice-married Mrs Simpson, which began when he was still Prince of Wales, was an open secret for years within the Royal Family, the Establishment, and café society circles in London, New York, and the capitals of Europe. Yet incredibly, even when it had progressed to the stage where American newspapers were openly predicting 'King to marry "Wally"' — and naming the date — all mention of the royal romance was deliberately withheld from the ordinary people of Great Britain until the constitutional crisis it had engendered reached flashpoint; a cover-up without precedent in the nation's history. Then, unable to have the woman of his choice proclaimed Queen at his forthcoming Coronation, denied the alternative of a morganatic marriage, and presented by his ministers with the stark choice of renouncing either the woman he loved or the Crown, the King chose to abdicate in favour of his brother Albert, Duke of York (later George VI). The former King sailed into exile on the night of 11 December 1936, aboard a British destroyer, after addressing the nation by radio. He married Mrs Simpson in France at the Château de Candé, near Tours, in June 1937. No member of the British royal family attended the wedding and most of his former friends stayed away. The service was conducted by an unknown, volunteer Anglican priest from Darlington.

On his wedding eve, the ex-King was officially informed that while he would henceforth be styled His Royal Highness the Duke of Windsor, the magic initials HRH were to be denied his wife, the Duchess – 'a damnable wedding present', he called it. For the rest of their lives together (the Duke died of cancer in May 1972) the Windsors remained objects of curiosity – and gossip – wherever they went.

Prince Edward was born to be King on 23 June 1894, the eldest son of George V and Queen Mary, at White Lodge, Richmond Park. He was christened Edward Albert Christian George Andrew Patrick David (but known to his family simply as 'David'). Mrs Simpson was born on 19 June 1896 at Blue Ridge Summit, Pennsylvania, USA, and christened Bessie Wallis (Warfield) – she was known throughout her childhood as 'Bessiewallis'. Both her parents came from good stock contrary to scurrilous rumour, once her name became linked with the King's. Her mother was a Montague from Baltimore, of Virginian ancestry and her father Teackle Wallis Warfield from Maryland. Both were of British descent.

'David' became the most popular Prince of Wales in history, idolized not only in Britain but throughout the Dominions and Empire. He travelled extensively as heir to the throne, winning instant acclaim with his good looks and boyish charm from the crowds who welcomed him everywhere. Bessie Wallis Warfield's father died at twenty-seven, leaving very little money. Mother and daughter moved to

Baltimore, where relatives paid Bessie's board-school fees. The widowed Mrs Warfield remarried in 1908, and, following the death of her second husband, for a third time in 1926.

In 1916 Bessie Wallis Warfield met and married her first husband, US Navy pilot Lieutenant Earl Winfield Spencer, Jr. They separated five years later and she was granted a divorce in 1927. That petition was already pending when she met the man who was to become her second husband and accompany her into the pages of history — Ernest Aldrich Simpson. His mother was American, his father an Englishman who headed a prosperous firm of shipbrokers with offices in New York and London. During World War I young Ernest Simpson sailed for London to enlist in the British forces; in June 1918 he was commissioned in the Coldstream Guards (but did not serve in France). His own first marriage, to divorcee Mrs Dorothy Parsons Dechert, also ended in divorce; that suit, too, was pending when he met Mrs Wallis Warfield Spencer in 1926. Both went separately to Europe in 1928, when they met in London and were married at the Chelsea registrar's office on 21 July.

The Simpsons' flat in Bryanston Court became a rendez-vous for businessmen, diplomats and influential journalists, and for the first years their marriage was a happy one. Husband and wife were introduced to the Prince of Wales in the winter of 1930, at a cocktail party given by Thelma, Lady Furness, at her home in Grosvenor Square.

The Prince of Wales fell in love three times before he was forty, on each occasion with someone else's wife. The first was Mrs Freda Dudley Ward, wife of Liberal Whip, William Dudley Ward, MP. She was caught in an air raid in 1918 as she was being escorted through Belgrave Square, in London, and sought refuge in a house there. Among those in the cellar which served as makeshift air raid shelter was the young Prince of Wales, on leave from France (where he served as staff officer). It was the beginning of a romance which lasted sixteen years and – by astonishing coincidence – the hostess who introduced them was the then unknown Ernest Simpson's married sister. Mrs Dudley Ward took an entirely practical view of her own affair with the Prince and wrote later: 'I never met either the King or the Queen. They regarded me as a scarlet woman. They were always after David to leave me and marry within his rank – some Princess or other. . . . Heavens, it wasn't as if I were *trying* to marry David! Or even wanted to. He asked me often enough, ardently too. But just as often I said no . . . the whole idea was ridiculous. I was already married, of course, so there'd have to be a divorce, and his parents and friends and the Church would never have allowed it . . .'

The Prince's second love was Thelma, Lady Furness. She was an American who had eloped at sixteen, divorced her first husband, and married again at twenty-one to the widowed Marmaduke, Viscount Furness, the shipping magnate. (They, too, were divorced in 1933). She had known the Prince of Wales for more than two years when he gave the Simpsons a lift home, from a party at the Furness house, early in 1931. Soon the Prince was a regular visitor to Bryanston Court and in January 1932 he invited the Simpsons to join him as his guests at Fort Belvedere, his residence on the outskirts of Windsor Great Park.

In the autumn of 1933, when Thelma, Lady Furness, sailed for New York, she asked her friend Wallis Simpson to 'look after' the Prince while she was away. By the time she returned to London the following spring, the Prince had become infatuated with Mrs Simpson. Angered by reports of Thelma, Lady Furness's friendship with Prince Aly Khan, he soon broke with her. His final break with Mrs Freda Dudley Ward came at about the same time, as he fell more and more under Wallis Simpson's influence.

Royal biographer Frances Lady Donaldson wrote of this period: 'Within a matter of weeks more gossip and scandal had been created than in the whole of his previous forty

Thelma Furness

years. Until now . . . there is no doubt that the Prince had added more to the brilliance of the Crown, to the magic of the monarchy, than he had taken away. From now on he was to behave with a senseless recklessness in minor matters, an imperviousness to other people's opinions and feelings, which, carelessly and publicly proclaimed, could not for long have been covered by his Household and must in the end have undermined even his extraordinary popularity . . .'

In August 1934 the Prince invited both Simpsons to join him on holiday at Biarritz. Ernest Simpson declined because of business commitments. Mrs Simpson, who was therefore obliged to decline also, later changed her mind and travelled to Biarritz with her aunt, Mrs Bessie Merryman, as chaperone. From Biarritz the Prince's party set sail on *Rosaura*, a yacht owned by Lord Moyne (of the Guinness family), for a fortnight's Mediterranean cruise. In the Duchess of Windsor's own words years later, it was on this cruise that her association with the Prince '. . . crossed the line that marks the indefinable boundary between friendship and love'. On their arrival at Cannes he gave her a diamond and emerald bracelet charm, the first in a cascade of precious stones he was to lavish on his new love.

The Prince holidayed twice in Europe in 1935, the first time at winter sports in Kitzbuhel, followed by a visit to Vienna and Budapest, then a leisurely summer vacation spent in the South of France, Switzerland, Austria and Hungary. On each occasion, both Simpsons were invited to join him. Each time Ernest Simpson declined while his wife accepted – and the inevitable scandal grew. The second time Ernest Simpson sailed for America to discuss his crumbling marriage with his wife's aunt, Mrs Merryman. At Balmoral, George V met with the Archbishop of Canterbury, the lugubrious Cosmo Lang, to mull over the situation. In a later talk with his Prime Minister, Stanley Baldwin, the King predicted with uncanny accuracy, 'After

The King and Mrs Simpson

I'm dead the boy will ruin himself in twelve months.' He died on 20 January 1936; David became King Edward VIII – and was on his way into exile, as ex-King, within the year.

Some observers, like his aide and cousin Lord Louis Mountbatten, always maintained that the Prince would have liked to discuss the possibility of marriage to Mrs Simpson during the King's lifetime, but was too much in awe of his disciplinarian father to do so. Once he was King himself, he was free to marry whom he wished within the bounds of the Royal Marriages Act. Given all that, there was still one major obstacle to overcome before he could entertain any hope of marrying Mrs Simpson: the fact that she was already married. At what stage the first steps were taken to obtain that essential divorce – and at whose instigation – has always been a subject of debate. Under the divorce laws then obtaining in England, a successful appellant would first be granted a decree nisi. (Literally 'nisi' means unless). Then, if no evidence was brought within six months to warrant the attention of the King's Proctor – evidence of collusion, perhaps, or some miscarriage of justice – the decree became absolute and both parties would be free to remarry. That unavoidable six months' interval would inevitably have been an important consideration if, as some were beginning to suspect and fear, the King intended to have Mrs Simpson crowned Queen on 12 May 1937, the date set for his Coronation.

American authors J. Bryan III and Charles J.V. Murphy state categorically in their book *The Windsor Story* that: '. . . the King stage-managed the divorce from beginning to end. Wallis's attitude was depicted in her bland assurance . . . a few months later . . . that the divorce was "at Ernest's instigation", and at no wish of hers. Precisely when the King decided to start preparations for her suit is not clear. The vague, but best available, date is "one evening in February 1936".' A close friend revealed that he was present, at Ernest Simpson's request, at a meeting between the two

125

men at the time. He said Simpson asked the King, 'Are you sincere? Do you intend to marry her?' and the King replied, 'Do you really think I would be crowned without Wallis by my side?' At that, say the authors: 'The bargain was struck. And kept.'

Certainly the King's subsequent conduct would appear to indicate that henceforth he took marriage to Mrs Simpson almost for granted, although there has never been any suggestion that either his own or Mrs Simpson's legal advisers were in any way involved. On 27 May 1936 he gave a dinner party at St James's Palace. The guests included the Mountbattens, Prime Minister Stanley Baldwin and his wife, the Duff Coopers and the Simpsons, husband and wife. Years later, as the Duchess of Windsor, she wrote that the King said he was inviting the Baldwins that night because 'Sooner or later my Prime Minister must meet my future wife . . .' What is beyond dispute, in the light of the divorce action that was then being prepared, is that the King's Mediterranean cruise that summer, with Mrs Simpson in the royal party but not her husband, was positively reckless, so much international publicity and speculation did it arouse.

Before the King left Britain, the Palace asked Fleet Street to respect his privacy on holiday, as usual. No such obligation rested upon the American and European press however. Unfortunately no one could accuse the King of discretion. First he hired a 250-foot luxury yacht, the *Nahlin*, complete with crew of fifty. When the royal party sailed in her from the Jugoslav port of Sibenik, with two Royal Navy destroyers in attendance, a crowd of many thousands turned up to see them off, shouting *Zivila Ljubav!* ('Long live love!'). Wherever they went the King and Mrs Simpson were photographed together; in Greek waters, at Instanbul, where they were fêted by Turkish dictator Kemal Ataturk, at every stop on their long return journey across Europe by train. True to its word, the British

Edward VIII and the Abdication Crisis – Behind The Scenes

The eccentric Bloomsbury hostess, Lady Ottoline Morrell, kept abreast of the 1930s social scene as well as the activities of all the literary lions she entertained at her home. In her journal in 1936 she recorded her chagrin that she and Virginia Woolf, her novelist friend, were not invited to a lunch with Mrs Wallace Simpson that had been arranged by Margot Asquith – 'It wouldn't do my dear,' said Margot, 'You see, she has never opened a book in her life . . .'

'All England and the Commonwealth live in terror that he will marry her. She isn't a bad sort I hear but very common,' reported Ottoline in her journal.

Later as the abdication crisis deepened, she set down what she heard on the social grapevine about all the stresses the King was suffering – trying to cope with his constitutional responsibilities and more private obligations.

'It is said that he is very nearly mad. He had injections to make himself more virile and they affected his head and have made him very violent. He has remained shut up at Fort Belvedere . . . Poor little fellow – they also say that he has been drinking all these last weeks and has signed two abdications and torn them up.'

Press, almost alone, made no open reference to Mrs Simpson's presence, although *The Times* was stung into commenting that a sovereign '. . . should be invested with a certain detachment and dignity . . .' Authors Bryan and Murphy summed up by saying: 'The King returned to London no longer the invincible figure he had appeared when he left to join the *Nahlin*. The world publicity had done for him. Within the Establishment, his reputation was in ruins . . .'

Back in Britain, Mrs Simpson's name then appeared in the Court Circular as one of the King's house guests at Balmoral. On this occasion, however, it was not only members of his family and the Establishment who were offended; now it was the turn of the public. The King had been asked earlier, by the trustees of the Royal Infirmary at Aberdeen, to open a new hospital extension on his arrival on Deeside. He had refused on the grounds that the Court would still be in mourning for his dead father. Since then he had been seen at Ascot and holidayed on the *Nahlin*; now, on the day that his brother, the Duke of York, deputized for him at Aberdeen, the King drove to Ballater railway station to meet Mrs Simpson on arrival there. This royal snub caused deep resentment, not only in Deeside but wherever the incident was related, in Scotland and south of the Border.

Soon after the King's return from Balmoral to London, a date was set for the hearing of the Simpson divorce action – 27 October. Already the American newspapers were showing an almost obsessive interest in the royal romance. Those papers were finding their way into Britain and the Dominions, and angry letters of protest were reaching the leaders of the Establishment in London, at Downing Street, Lambeth Palace and the Foreign Office. Behind the scenes, pressure grew to try to have the divorce proceedings stopped but the King would have none of it. He told Prime Minister Baldwin that the divorce was the lady's private business, adding, 'It would be wrong were I to attempt to influence Mrs Simpson just because . . . she happens to be a friend.'

On 12 October 1936 Lord Beaverbrook, Canadian proprietor of the all-powerful *Express* group of newspapers, learned that the divorce was to be heard at Ipswich. He thereupon rang Mrs Simpson's solicitor, Theodore Goddard, and told him he intended to publish a report on the forthcoming petition in the *Evening Standard*. Goddard then called personally on Beaverbrook, to deny that the King intended to marry Mrs Simpson. Later the King invited Lord Beaverbrook to call on him and asked him not only to suppress all comment before the case was heard but for his help in 'limiting publicity' afterwards, on the grounds that Mrs Simpson was 'ill, unhappy and distressed by the thought of notoriety . . . Notoriety would attach to her only because she had been his guest on the *Nahlin* and at Balmoral'.

Lord Beaverbrook agreed and together with Esmond Harmsworth (son of Lord Rothermere, owner of the *Daily Mail* group), persuaded the rest of the British Press to agree to this unprecedented voluntary pact of silence. Beaverbrook wrote later that: 'While I was engaged in these activities directed to regulating publicity, I had no knowledge that marriage was in the mind of the King. He himself had given me no hint of the matter, and, at the same time, I had been told by Mrs Simpson's solicitor, Mr Theodore Goddard, that His Majesty had no such intention. I repeated that assurance to other newspaper proprietors. And I believed it . . .'

The divorce was heard at Ipswich where Mrs Simpson had taken up residence, presumably as a further deterrent to possible publicity. She was awarded a decree nisi against her husband, with costs, on the grounds of his adultery (with a professional co-respondent called Buttercup Kennedy but not named in court). As the former Mrs Simpson left with her solicitor, Theodore Goddard, so the courtroom doors were locked to keep the Press inside. Outside, two photographers had their cameras smashed by the police as they attempted to photograph her. In the confusion, the King's chauffeur drove off with Mrs Simpson: yet next morning, as agreed, the divorce proceedings were reported without comment.

Queen Elizabeth I, known as the Virgin Queen, is in fact believed to have had several lovers. One of the oddest was Francis, Duke of Alencon. The Duke, once described as a 'hideous dwarf', had suffered from smallpox which had stunted his growth and scarred his body. As a result of the disease, his nose had divided down the middle and pointed in two distinct directions. This, his enemies said, was symbolic of his two-facedness. Francis' weird physique and bumpy skin led Elizabeth to nickname him her 'petit grenouille', or little frog.

On 13 November, after a visit to the Fleet at Southampton — where he was given a rousing ovation — the King returned to Fort Belvedere to find a terse, coldly polite letter awaiting him from his Private Secretary, Major Alexander Hardinge. In it the King was warned that the Press was about to break its pact of silence and told that Prime Minister Baldwin had called a Cabinet to decide what action should be taken 'to deal with the serious situation which is developing'. Hardinge spoke of the possible resignation of the government and the damage which could result from an Election fought on the issue of the King's private life. His letter ended: 'If Your Majesty will permit me to say so, there is only one step which holds out any prospect of avoiding this dangerous situation, and that is for Mrs Simpson to go

abroad *without further delay* and I would beg your Majesty
to give this proposal your earnest consideration before the
situation has become irretrievable . . .'

The King met with Prime Minister Baldwin and was told
that his marriage to Mrs Simpson would not meet with the
approval of the Cabinet. The King's response was that his mind
was made up and that he was ready to abdicate if need be to
marry her. Baldwin called it 'grievous news'. Later Queen
Mary, Edward's mother, wrote to her son saying: 'I do not
think you have ever realized the shock which the attitude you
took up caused your family and the whole nation . . . It seemed
inconceivable to those who had made such sacrifices during the
war that you, as their King, refused a lesser sacrifice . . .'

By now gossip was rife in the Commons. MPs, already
restive under the self-imposed Press censorship, were
becoming increasingly concerned with the government's
own deliberate attempts to hide the truth from the people.
On 17 November 1936 Socialist MP Ellen Wilkinson put a
leading question to Sir Walter Runciman, President of the
Board of Trade, 'Can the Right Honourable Gentleman say
why, in the case of two American magazines of the highest
repute imported into this country in the last few weeks, two
and sometimes three pages have been torn out; and what is
this thing the British public are not allowed to know?' To
which Runciman replied equivocally, 'My department has
nothing to do with that . . .'

Next day the King put private cares aside, and carried out
the tour by which he is still best remembered in Britain –
through the distressed areas of the Rhondda and Mon-
mouth valleys of South Wales. The unemployed, who knew
nothing of the pending crisis, turned out in their thousands
to cheer him and sing hymns of praise in Welsh. The King,
who was deeply and visibly moved, declared passionately
as he looked at all the poverty around him that, 'Something
must be done.' If it was an empty promise, it was still the
charismatic King at his best, establishing instant rapport

with his subjects, so that he and his closest advisers were greatly impressed by the obvious public support he commanded.

Equally, no one who was aware of the fast-approaching constitutional crisis wanted the King to go, but most were determined that Mrs Simpson should not become Queen of England. Their objections had nothing to do with the fact that she was an American, or a commoner; they were that she was a twice-divorced woman, with her two ex-husbands still alive. Similarly, even those who supported the King's desire to marry the woman of his choice, believed his best course was not to challenge the Establishment head-on but to proceed with his Coronation and then, at some unspecified future date, when Mrs Simpson had won public approval by example, to raise the issue again. This was unacceptable to the King, who felt it meant 'being crowned with a lie on my lips'. Instead, he approved the suggestion of a morganatic marriage, which meant that Mrs Simpson would become Consort of lesser rank (possibly Duchess), and with a proviso that their children if any could not enter the line of succession.

Again Prime Minister Baldwin, who knew what the answer must be, tried to dissuade the King from forcing the issue. He pointed out that the morganatic marriage proposal would have to be put, not only to the Cabinet at home but also to the governments of the Dominions. (Under the terms of the Statute of Westminster of 1931, '. . . any alteration in the law touching the Succession to the Throne or the Royal Style and Titles, shall hereafter require assent as well of the Parliaments of all the Dominions as of the Parliament of the United Kingdom.') Baldwin then asked the King if that was his wish: the answer was 'yes' and at once abdication loomed that much closer.

Lord Beaverbrook, who had been recalled from a trans-Atlantic holiday by the King, immediately advised him to withdraw his request. Beaverbrook realized that if Baldwin's

The Duke of Windsor and Wallis Simpson on their wedding day, 1937

cabinet colleagues advised against a morganatic marriage — and the King refused to accept that advice — then his ministers would have to resign. A General Election would then be fought on the very issue Hardinge had warned against, the King's marriage to twice-divorced Mrs Simpson and the title she should assume. However, after Lord Beaverbrook was telephoned by the King late that night and told, 'Mrs Simpson . . . prefers the morganatic marriage to any other solution . . .' he realized the battle was lost.

Baldwin, who was later accused of slanting the vital telegrams to the Dominion Prime Ministers, received the answer he expected. None was in favour of the morganatic marriage proposal, although some were less emphatic than others. From talks with Opposition leader Clement Attlee, Baldwin also knew that, with the exception of a few back-benchers, Parliament at home was against it. Since the voluntary 'Pact of Silence' still held in the Press, however, there had been no opportunity to sound out public opinion as late as the end of November. Then dramatically — and in all innocence, he later claimed — the silence was broken by the Bishop of Bradford, Dr Alfred Blunt, in an address to his diocesan conference. After a reference to the essential religious nature of the Coronation ceremony, the aptly-named Bishop went on to say, 'The benefit of the King's Coronation depends under God upon two elements — firstly, on the faith, prayer and self-dedication of the King himself. On that it would be improper for me to say anything except to commend him, and ask others to commend him, to God's grace, which he will so abundantly need — for the King is a man like any other — if he is to do his duty properly. We hope he is aware of this need. Some of us wish that he gave more positive signs of such awareness . . .'

Although Dr Blunt later protested that at the time he had not heard of Mrs Simpson, the Press clearly thought otherwise. The provincial newspapers examined the speech first. 'Dr Blunt must have good reason for so pointed a remark', insisted the influential *Yorkshire Post*. 'Most people by this time are aware that a good deal of rumour regarding the King has been published of late in the more sensational American newspapers . . . But certain comments which have appeared in reputable United States journals, and even we believe in some Dominions newspapers, cannot be treated with quite so much indifference. They are too circumstantial, and plainly have a foundation in fact . . .'

On the same morning the *Yorkshire Post* was published, the Cabinet in London formally rejected the proposal of a morganatic marriage between the King and Mrs Simpson. Prime Minister Baldwin called on the King that night to discuss the situation. In their varying accounts later of what took place at that meeting, both parties agreed on one thing: that Baldwin urged the King not to abdicate. However, he was obliged to point out that the King had three courses only left open to him. They were: to give up the idea of marriage to Mrs Simpson altogether, to marry against his government's advice – and plunge the country into constitutional crisis – or to abdicate, and marry. As the King considered his position, so Fleet Street joined in the great debate, at long last. Press reaction in the critical week that followed was mixed, with more newspapers against the marriage than for it. In the end the King, disheartened by Press comment generally, and increasingly worried by anonymous threats made against Mrs Simpson, arranged for her to leave for the South of France accompanied by his Lord in Waiting, Lord Brownlow, and his personal body-guard.

Before she left, Mrs Simpson suggested the King might borrow an idea from the American presidency and discuss his dilemma with his subjects direct – through a 'fireside chat' broadcast. The King was enthusiastic but when he showed the proposed draft to Baldwin, the Premier warned him that, although he was willing to discuss the idea with his ministerial colleagues, he was in no doubt what their decision would be. He further pointed out that any such appeal to the public, over the heads of the elected government, would be unconstitutional. (Baldwin's opponents later claimed that he had already discussed the draft with his Cabinet who rejected it before he called on the King).

According to Baldwin, the King replied, 'You want me to go, don't you? And before I go, I think it is right for her sake and mine that I should speak.' To which the Premier responded, 'What I want, Sir, is what you told me you wanted: to go with dignity, not dividing the country, and making things as smooth as possible for your successor . . . You will be telling millions throughout the world – among them a vast number of women – that you are determined to marry one who has a husband living . . . You may, by speaking, divide opinion; but you will certainly harden it.'

Shortly afterwards the King left Buckingham Palace for the last time as sovereign and drove to Fort Belvedere. As always in critical moments in the nation's history, crowds began to gather outside the Palace and Number 10, Downing Street. Denied information for so long by Press silence, their understandable confusion was reflected in the placards they carried: some for, some against the marriage. 'After South Wales, You Can't Let Him Down . . . Come To The Palace Now!' Opponents of the marriage in their turn spread the crudest anti-Simpson jokes. 'Heard about the King's new job? He wants to sign on as Third Mate on an American tramp!'

On 4 December, Baldwin told the House bluntly that there was no such thing as morganatic marriage in English law. 'The lady whom [the King] marries . . . necessarily becomes Queen. The only way in which this result could be avoided would be by legislation dealing with a particular case. His Majesty's Government are not prepared to introduce such legislation.' According to the *Daily Telegraph* (which was pro-Baldwin) the Prime Minister was cheered so loudly at this, 'that for a little while, [he] could not continue . . .' Mrs Simpson telephoned from France and urged the King to 'fight for his rights', but all to no avail. On the morning of 5 December he sent Walter Monckton, his barrister friend and adviser, to Downing Street to inform Baldwin officially that he intended to abdicate. When Beaverbrook heard the news he told Winston Churchill, the King's political champion, 'Our cock won't fight.' On 7 December Churchill himself was howled down in the Commons when he sought an assurance from Baldwin that no 'irrevocable' step should be taken by the government. Behind the scenes there were real fears that the King's Proctor might yet be asked to intervene and quash the decree nisi awarded to Mrs Simpson (and so thwart the intended marriage), but an attempt to have the divorce made absolute forthwith by Act of Parliament was resisted by the government, who believed that any such Bill could only provoke an even greater scandal.

Desperate eleventh-hour attempts were made to try to prevent the abdication. In Cannes, Mrs Simpson (under pressure, it was said, from Lord Brownlow) put out a Press statement which read: 'Mrs Simpson, throughout the last few weeks, has invariably wished to avoid any action or proposal which would hurt or damage His Majesty or the Throne. Today her attitude is unchanged and she is willing, if such action would solve the problem, to withdraw from a situation that has been rendered both unhappy and untenable.' When told of its contents, the King, who was anxious that she should not be blamed for the crisis, said simply, 'Go ahead if you wish. But it won't make any difference.' Shortly afterwards Mrs Simpson's solicitor, Theodore Goddard, flew to Cannes to call on his client. Different reasons have since been given for his visit. One was that he had learned that an affidavit was about to be served on the King's Proctor, allegedly accompanied by 'evidence' of collusion, by a private individual. Another, widely circulated within the Establishment, was that he had been requested to recover jewellery left by Queen Alexandra (wife of Edward VII), and since given to Mrs Simpson by the King. In the event, Mr Goddard telephoned the following message to the Prime Minister, after meeting with Mrs Simpson in Cannes: 'I have today discussed the whole position with Mrs Simpson – her own, the position of the King, the country, the Empire. Mrs Simpson tells me she was, and still is, perfectly willing to instruct me to withdraw her petition for divorce and willing to do anything to prevent the King from abdicating. I am satisfied that this is Mrs Simpson's genuine and honest desire. I read this note over to Mrs Simpson who in every way confirmed it.' It was signed by Mr Goddard, and counter-signed by Lord Brownlow.

In their turn the Cabinet sent a formal message to the King, asking him to reconsider his intention to abdicate. This he refused to do. 'His Majesty has given the matter his further consideration but regrets he is unable to alter his decision.' All that remained now was for the parties concerned to settle the King's future finances (never officially disclosed but said to be very considerable) and his rank. On Thursday, 10 December he signed the Instrument of Abdication. It read: 'I, Edward the Eighth, of Great Britain, Ireland, and the British Dominions beyond the Seas, King, Emperor of India, do hereby declare My irrevocable determination to renounce the Throne for Myself and My descendants . . .' It was witnessed by his three brothers, Albert (York), Henry (Gloucester) and George (Kent).

On 11 December he sailed into exile. Only now that he was ex-King could he broadcast to his former subjects without first seeking government sanction. However, as a matter of courtesy, he sent an advance copy of his farewell speech to No. 10 Downing Street. Walter Monckton drove with him from Fort Belvedere to Windsor Castle, whence

The Duke and Duchess of Windsor

the broadcast was to be made. Sir John Reith, Director General of the BBC, introduced him, on the personal instructions of the new King, his brother George VI, as 'His Royal Highness Prince Edward'. It was a moving, memorable speech and occasion, and his voice was heard wherever English was spoken:

'You all know the reasons which have impelled me to renounce the Throne. But I want you to understand that in making up my mind I did not forget the country or the Empire which as Prince of Wales, and lately as King, I have for twenty-five years tried to serve. But you must believe me when I tell you that I have found it impossible to carry the heavy burden of responsibility and to discharge my duties as King as I would wish to do, without the help and support of the woman I love'.

Authors Bryan and Murphy described the scene 3,000 miles from Windsor Castle: 'In New York, taxi drivers pulled over to the kerb and stopped, to hear him through. The whole English-speaking world all but stood still for seventy seconds. People wept. There never has been its match for pathos: a king – a King of England! – renouncing his imperial splendour for love alone . . .'

Chapter Nine

THE BUCKINGHAM PALACE SECURITY SCANDAL

House break-ins have become so common in London
that it has become a genuine oddity to see one
reported in the media. Yet in the summer of 1982 one
particular break-in caused such a furore that questions were
asked in the House of Commons and calls were made for
the resignations of both the Chief of the Metropolitan
Police and the Home Secretary. Oddly enough, the cause of
so much fuss was not a burglar or a spy, but an unemployed
labourer trying to do Queen Elizabeth a favour.

Thirty-two-year-old Michael Fagan broke into Buckingham Palace *twice* in the months of June and July 1982 and
might have gone undetected both times if he had not felt it
was his duty to tell Her Majesty that her palace security
was shockingly poor.

Fagan later claimed that he had noticed that Buckingham
Palace's security was 'a bit lax' during a sightseeing trip
with his two young children. He became increasingly
disturbed by this risk to the Royal family – for whom he
had great admiration – and eventually decided to break into
the palace as an act of public-spiritedness. 'I wanted to
prove the Queen was not too safe,' he said later.

Fagan must also have been inspired by the fact that a
year before, in the summer of 1981, three West Germans
had been found peacefully camping in the palace grounds.
When questioned by police they said that they had arrived

in London late at night and had climbed over the palace railings in the belief they were entering a public park. They had camped there totally undisturbed until the next morning. A rueful palace spokesman later admitted that this was not the first time that this sort of thing had happened.

On the night of 7 June 1982, Fagan clambered over the iron railings that surround the palace and wandered into Ambassadors Court. Here he found a sturdy drain pipe and proceeded to shin his way up to the roof. On the way he paused to look in at a lighted window. The occupant, housemaid Sarah Jane Carter, was reading in bed and happened to look up when Fagan was looking in. He moved on quickly and the housemaid, shaken and partially convinced that she had been seeing things, called security. They decided not to investigate.

After climbing fifty feet — no small feat in the dark — Fagan reached a flat roof that adjoined the royal apartments. He opened a window and climbed in. Over the next half hour he wandered about quite freely, crossing several infrared security beams as he did so. These had been fitted incorrectly, like the window alarm, and failed to go off.

During his walk-about he paused to admire the various royal portraits and had a brief rest on the throne. He also came across some royal bedrooms — those of Mark Phillips and the Duke of Edinburgh — the first he decided not to bother and the second turned out to be elsewhere. He then entered the Post Room and found a fridge containing a bottle of Californian white wine. Expecting to be arrested at any moment he decided to relax a bit first. He had drunk half the bottle by the time he realized that nobody was coming to get him, so he put it down and left by the risky way he had entered.

Just over a month later, on the night of 9 July, he drank a fair amount of whisky and set out to repeat his performance. Once again he entered the palace with no difficulties. This time though, he was clearly suffering from stress and too much booze. He smashed a royal ash-tray with the intent of cutting his wrists with the jagged edge, but in doing so cut his hand. Thus, looking for a suitable place to kill himself and dripping blood on the carpet, he came across a door that pronounced itself to be the entry to the Queen's bedroom.

Her Majesty awoke to find Michael Fagan sitting on the edge of her bed, nursing his wounded hand and mumbling in a quiet voice. Speaking reassuringly to him she quietly reached for the alarm button by her bed, but unfortunately it had been incorrectly wired and failed to work. When she realized that nobody was coming, she marshalled considerable courage and picked up the bedside telephone — this apparently didn't bother Fagan in the least. The telephone connected her directly to the palace switchboard and she asked them to put her through to security. Unfortunately the police guard had already finished for the night and nobody else in the vicinity could be raised. Her footman was out in the grounds walking the royal corgis and the nightmaid was working in a room out of earshot of a telephone. The Queen kept a brave face in what must have been a nightmare situation and kept on chatting with the intruder.

Eventually Fagan asked for a cigarette and the Queen, pointing out she was a non-smoker, said she would go and get one from a member of staff. By this time the footman, Paul Whybrew, had returned from walking the dogs and quickly went in to confront the intruder. Fagan quietly insisted that all he wanted to do was talk with *his* Queen. Whybrew said that was fine, but in all fairness he should let her get dressed first. Fagan agreed and went with the footman and a maid to a nearby pantry. He waited there quietly until the police eventually arrived and arrested him.

Despite the fact that Michael Fagan gave a full and detailed confession of both break-ins, the police and crown prosecution faced a difficult problem. It is a peculiarity of

English law that entering another person's property is not a criminal offence unless it can be proved that it was done with an intent to commit a crime (Fagan could have been charged with trespassing, but that would have merely been a civil offence). Thus, rather ridiculously, Fagan was tried in the Old Bailey for the theft of half a bottle of wine (valued by the court at £3) that was technically owned by the Prince and Princess of Wales.

The trial contained some farcical scenes. When Mrs Barbra Mills, acting for the prosecution asked Fagan: 'It wasn't your drink was it?' He replied: 'It wasn't my palace either.' 'It was not your right to drink it,' she insisted, to which Fagan countered: 'Well, I'd done a hard day's work for the Queen, showing her how to break her security.' He went on to point out that Her Majesty was lucky that somebody as public-spirited as himself had broken into her apartments; 'I mean, I could have been a rapist or something!'

The jury acquitted Fagan of the crime of theft, but he was held in custody on an unconnected charge of taking and driving away a car without the owner's permission, to which he had also admitted. His second trial took place that October and after he had pleaded guilty, the judge ordered him to be placed in the care of a high security mental hospital. Despite the fact that it was pressed by several doctors that he should be held without time limit, he was given the right to appeal.

In January of the following year the psychiatric review board found that he was 'not fully recovered', but on the grounds that he offered no threat to the community allowed his release. Perhaps predictably, angry questions were asked in the House of Commons.

The mortified police officers in charge of palace security might have hoped for a bit of peace and quiet in which to put their house in order, but this was not to be. Fagan's break-in indirectly sparked-off another, if unconnected, scandal involving one of their most senior officers.

Dining with the Queen

Michael Holroyd, the biographer, was once invited to a state banquet with members of the royal family. He was very well positioned, opposite one particularly distinguished lady member of the clan. She began to demonstrate a great ability to mimic accents.

First she did an incredibly accurate imitation of a Yorkshire accent. Michael Holroyd clapped in admiration. Next she managed an absolutely perfect rendition of an Irish lilt. Mr Holroyd murmured in anticipation. Her powers of mime were truly wonderful. Finally she did a third accent, quite brilliantly, and the biographer had to burst into spontaneous applause. He burst out laughing and congratulated Her Majesty heartily. Now that one, he commented, was truly superb. An absolutely priceless imitation of an accent. The table fell silent and the lady stared. She had been speaking in her own voice.

Chapter Ten

ANNUS HORRIBILIS

Prince Charles, Lady Diana
and Other Royal Scandals

750 million people watched the marriage of Prince
Charles, the Prince of Wales to Lady Diana Spencer
on 29 July, 1981. A frenzy of media attention had
surrounded the ceremony. The diffident bride-to-be
had been pursued everywhere by gangs of reporters.
The natural curiosity of the British public was fed by
daily stories in competing tabloid newspapers. In the
battle for circulation each one was desperate to outdo the
others with pictures of the couple taken in private, or
stories of their courtship wheedled from close friends.
Diana's face smiled from the cover of nearly every
magazine on the news stands.

The British public's delight at the prospect of a royal
wedding was mingled with relief. During the late seventies,
Charles' name had been linked in the press with many
eligible socialites – Davina Sheffield, Princess Marie-Astrid
of Luxembourg, Susan George, Sabrina Guinness, Amanda
Knatchbull, Anna Wallace, Jane Ward – the latter the
manageress at the Guards Polo Club where the Prince
regularly played – but every time the gossip column
writers predicted that a royal wedding was in the offing,
their hopes had been frustrated. 'Sources' close to the prince
would report that the relationship was over, or had never
even happened. The general opinion among royal obser-

vers was that Charles, at 31, was taking rather longer than necessary to sow his wild oats.

So when his engagement to Diana was announced on 24 February, 1981, the same royal observers agreed that his choice was showed excellent taste. The bride to be was attractive, charmingly shy in front of the cameras, and most importantly, from the right background. Diana was the third daughter of Earl Spencer. In the tradition of the British royal family, she was not formidably intellectual – she had left school with only two 'O' levels, and had then taken a course in cookery, and worked as a child minder. Clearly Diana was not intended to take up a professional career. She had 'wife of the gentry' written all over her.

What no one realised until later was that Prince Charles himself was not entirely happy about the idea of marrying Diana Spencer. He had finally given way to family pressure to settle down and provide an heir – pressure from his mother and father, his Uncle Dickie (Lord Louis Mountbatten), and from the Queen Mother, who virtually chose Diana herself – a demure, compassionate girl with the right social background.

In fact, Diana had not had the happy, sheltered life everyone assumed. When she was three, her mother had fallen in love with another man, and the Spencers were divorced three years later. She had been brought up by her father. The divorce disturbed her deeply, and it may have been in reaction that she began to devote much attention to sick animals. It also seems to have been responsible for a tendency to overeat that made her plump and – to her own eyes – unattractive. As a teenager she had worked at a kindergarten in Pimlico, and shared a flat with three friends. But although she had boyfriends, she remained – according to her flatmates – sexually inexperienced; one commentator says this was because she saw sex as the cause of the breakup of her parents' marriage, and was afraid of it.

Charles, on the other hand, had had three serious sexual relationships in the year before the engagement was announced. Since the mid-1970s, many women had been to dinner in his flat in Buckingham Palace and stayed the night. The prince's valet, Stephen Barry, later told a gossip columnist how he had frequently retrieved items of ladies' underwear from under the bed or behind the cushions of the settee. If the owner was known, these were laundered and returned to the lady in an Asprey gift box; if not, they might be presented to members of the Palace staff — occasionally gentlemen. (The same gossip columnist remarks that many of the male staff at Buckingham Palace are homosexual, since homosexuals have no wives to divide their loyalties, and tend to enjoy the protocol of Palace life.) Prince Andrew is reported to have told a girlfriend that his brother was trying to emulate actor Warren Beatty, who had the reputation of having slept with every attractive starlet in Hollywood. According to gossip columnist Nigel Dempster, there was even a 'slush fund' that had been set up to pay off the women who objected to being one-night stands, a few of whom received a dollar cheque running to six figures. Unlike the Prince Regent, described in an earlier chapter, Charles seems to have had no problem financing his high turnover of mistresses.

Charles had also had a brief romance with Diana's sister Sarah (who later insisted it had remained platonic), and so the general assumption was that Diana had begun to feel an interest in Charles at this time — many girls develop a crush on their elder sister's boyfriends. (Sarah had apparently been finally rejected by Charles's 'vetters' because she suffered from anorexia and was a chain smoker — her sister called her 'fag-ash Lil'.) The only slight problem seemed to be the difference in their ages of Charles and Diana. At 20, Lady Di was more ten years younger then her royal husband-to-be.

> Enlil-Bani, ancient king of Babylonia, began life
> as the gardener of the previous king Erra-Imitti.
> According to tradition, each new year, a 'King
> for a Day' was chosen. A commoner took the
> throne for twenty-four hours, at the end of
> which, he was sacrificed to the gods. Enlil-Bani
> was selected for this dubious honour, but before
> the day was up, the true king dropped dead.
> The gardener continued his reign for at least
> twenty-four years afterwards.

On 29 July, 1981, St Paul's Cathedral was the focus of the world's attention. In the surrounding streets, many were unashamed to weep with joy at the sight of their future king and queen. When the couple kissed on the balcony of Buckingham Palace after the ceremony, the crowds that jammed the Mall screamed their approval. Despite the economic recession and Britain's declining importance in the league of world powers, the nation was proud; there had been nothing so romantic since Prince Rainier married Grace Kelly in Monaco.

Perhaps it was the feeling of anti-climax that followed the wedding that started the reaction. Newspapers that had whipped their readership into a frenzy of nationalism with massive souvenir pullouts and photo specials found it difficult to simply drop the story and return to more mundane and depressing news. Even if the newspapers' editors had wanted to, competition would not allow it. A paper with a new picture of Diana outsold its Dianaless rival. The publicity was unrelenting: every minor occasion at which the Prince and Princess of Wales appeared in public received blanket attention. In the frenzy of interest in the future queen, Charles was sometimes forgotten. At public appearances, it was clear who the crowds had turned out to see. Charles seemed to take the implied affront in good part, apologizing to crowds in Wales that he only had one wife.

Soon the purely descriptive news items, praising Diana's dress-sense and cooing about the happy couple, began to sound a little repetitive. Clearly, while the public's appetite for royal gossip was undiminished, every tabloid editor sensed that they were beginning to get bored with positive stories. To vary the diet, feature writers began turning out pieces expressing concern articles about Diana's well-being. They pointed out that in February, when the engagement was announced, Diana had been a rosy-cheeked, healthy looking girl who looked as if she played hockey every morning before breakfast. By the time of the wedding, she had shed considerable weight, and her cheeks were no longer so rosy. No doubt she had been dieting for her wedding day — but could it be that she was overdoing it?

When, in the months following the wedding, the princess seemed to go on losing weight, the newspapers clucked and worried like maiden aunts. Their anxiety communicated itself to the public, who responded by buying the newspapers that sounded most concerned. So when, on 21 November, 1981, the palace announced that Diana was pregnant, everyone heaved a sigh of relief — not least the newspaper editors, who now had an excuse for beginning the party all over again.

In February 1982, five months into Diana's pregnancy, the Wales' holidayed on Windermere Island in the Bahamas. For many years there had been an unspoken agreement between Fleet Street and the Palace that royal holidays were no-go areas. This tradition soon fell a victim to the circulation war, and newspaper photographers secretly photographed Diana in her bikini. These pictures revealed that, although pregnant, she was still obviously underweight.

The wedding of HRH Prince Charles and Lady Diana Spencer, 1981

The publication of these pictures brought a strong rebuke from the Palace. It was, said the spokesman, 'one of the blackest days in British journalism.' Such a criticism from the royal family was unheard of, mainly because long-established guidelines of good taste had previously governed what could be printed. But in Fleet Street times were changing. The struggle for circulation meant that such tacit agreements were luxuries that could no longer be afforded.

All this prying and intrusion involved a slow change in the attitude of reporters towards Prince Charles. Familiarity breeds contempt. The tacit agreement that had operated since the time of Queen Victoria meant that reporters addressed the Prince of Wales as 'sir' and treated him with respect. They continued to address him as 'sir', but the respect was eroding. Charles' admission that he talked to his plants in order to encourage them to grow resulted in acres of newsprint ridicule in the tabloids. Taken in combination with his avowed liking for the mystical writings of Sir Laurens Van Der Post, Charles was made to appear to be a kind of blue-blooded hippy. Yet he had many sympathizers when, in 1983, he attacked plans for an addition to the National Gallery in Trafalgar Square, describing it as a 'carbuncle on the face of a much-loved and elegant friend'. (The plans for the extension were then dropped).

The couple certainly had to endure trial-by-camera. Every time they appeared together, the expressions on their faces were analysed and discussed in the captions, and they sometimes they had to endure intrusions by long telephoto lenses. (Charles had been sensitive about such matters ever since he had been photographed, in May 1980, lying on a blanket by the river at Balmoral with a girlfriend named Anna Wallace.) Moreover, the smallest physical contact between Charles and any other woman who happened to be in the entourage was subjected to the same minute analysis.

There was also an attempt to 'humanise' the royal couple with 'chatty' (i.e. disrespectful) and 'homely' (impertinent) stories – for example, after the Wales' second son, Harry was born, the newspapers revealed that William and Harry were known by their parents as the 'heir and spare'.

Now in their fourth year of marriage, Charles and Diana were granted a respite. Finally starved of new material for gossip, the tabloids had turned their attention on to Prince Andrew, Charles' younger brother. Andrew's relationships with women provided more substantial fare than the diet of innuendo and rumour in the stories about Diana. Andrew was portrayed as libidinous and cheeky, a convenient contrast to the intellectual and contemplative Charles. Andrew played up to the 'Randy Andy' tag. He attempted to get TV presenter Selina Scott's phone number while being interviewed by her for Terry Wogan, and was often photographed 'out on the town' with one-time soft-porn actress Katherine 'Koo' Stark.

But by 1985, Andrew was 25, the age when royal tradition dictated that he should be thinking of marriage. Then, during the Royal Ascot week party at Windsor Castle, the invited guests were surprised to see Andrew hand-feeding profiteroles to the freckled and bouncy red-head who was seated next to him. The woman was Sarah Ferguson, daughter of Major Ronald Ferguson, Prince Charles' polo manager. Such open friskiness tied in well with Andrew's playboy image, and the papers immediately began to cover the couple's meetings extensively.

And meet they did, often and publicly. At the time of the Ascot party, Sarah had been the girlfriend of racing driver Paddy McNally. It was rumoured that, after giving Mac-Nally an ultimatum: 'Marry me or else . . .', Sarah had decisively dropped him. The palace plainly approved of 'Fergie' (as Sarah was known). It was, after all, the seating arrangements at a royal party that had brought them together. Such things are not random or accidental . . .

Andrew and Fergie's engagement was announced in February 1986, to no one's great surprise. Their wedding took place in Westminster Abbey in July of that year. Although not as grand an affair as the wedding of his elder brother, Andrew's wedding excited the same public enthusiasm. Fergie, of course, could hardly be less like Diana; where Diana's image was shy and demure, Fergie's was effervescent and mischievous. Everyone liked her — she looked as if she would enjoy a game of darts in the local pub. When newspapers reported that Diana and Fergie had dressed up as police women in order to gatecrash Andrew's stag night party, no one had any doubt who thought up the idea.

On his marriage, Andrew inherited the title of the Duke of York. The Queen's present to the couple was a lease on the Sunninghill estate, as well as the money to build a family house there.

The tone of the articles about the two royal couples became less and less positive as the decade wore on. The Duchess of York seemed to be permanently on holiday: she beamed from the ski-slopes or golden beaches at least once a week. Rightly or wrongly the British public suspected that it was their tax revenues that was enabling her to live this enviable life. The 'respectable' newspapers began to voice a certain irritation with the British obsession with the younger members of the royal family, and the *Independent* newspaper, which had just been established, expressed the broadsheets' boredom with royal stories by covering Beatrice's birth with a single line in the Births, Marriages and Deaths column in the back pages. Again, there was criticism when, after the birth of Princess Beatrice, the Duchess of York went off to join her husband in Australia, and yet again when she took her daughter skiing in Switzerland while she still had a chickenpox rash. Her plans for her new home in Berkshire were derided as vulgar and ostentatious.

Royal Scandals

What was worse, from the point of view of the royal family, was that it was very obvious that all was not well between Charles and Diana. She was blamed because members of Charles's household were said to have resigned because they found her too demanding. Even in the mid-80s it was noted that the couple seemed to spend little time together, and that they seemed to barely tolerate each other in public. The days of sunny smiles for the cameras seemed to be past.

By the late 1980s the tabloids were busy spreading doubts about the strength of both marriages. Prince Charles, they hinted regularly, was having an affair with Camilla Parker-Bowles, an old girlfriend now married. Fergie was also suspected of infidelity with Texan millionaire Steve Wyatt, her financial adviser. Yet no real evidence, apart from whispered confidences from sources 'close to Charles' or 'a Palace insider', were offered. But it seemed clear that the newspapers knew more than they were prepared to print; they regularly hinted that they could not tell the full truth.

Things began to fall apart for the Yorks in January 1992. Maurice Marple, a window cleaner, had been hired by an estate agent to clean a flat in Cadogan Square. While throwing out the unwanted property left by the previous tenant, Marple happened upon a thick stack of photos perched on top of a wardrobe. Idly flicking through them before consigning them to the black plastic sack, Marple suddenly recognised the face of the Duchess of York, Sarah Ferguson. Some of the photos showed the duchess and a handsome tanned man in swimsuits, laughing and having a good time. Others showed the unidentified man playing with Princess Beatrice, and riding a horse beside Fergie. What the other photos showed is not known.

Mr Marple decided that the newspapers would be interested in his discovery. He took them to the *Daily Mail*, who advised him to give them to the police. Whether he did this is not clear; all that *is* known is that some of the photographs were published in *Paris-Match*.

During the next few days the tabloids British made much of their restraint in not publishing the pictures. But they dropped very broad hints that the photos showed the duchess in inappropriate positions with a man identified as the Texan millionaire Steve Wyatt.

In fact, the affair had been known to all Fergie's friends for a long time. Wyatt was undoubtedly handsome, in a lean, Texan way, with very white teeth. He and Fergie had met in 1990, when Prince Andrew was away from home – in the navy – for all but forty-two nights of the year. She was pregnant when she visited Wyatt's ranch in Texas, but the affair progressed nevertheless. In a French Riviera restaurant with Fergie and Saddam Hussein's oil marketing chief (this was soon after Saddam's invasion of Kuwait), Wyatt embarrassed Lord McAlpine and his guests by pulling Fergie into his lap with the comment: 'Mah woman and I sit together.' Eventually, Fergie was persuaded by the queen and her own mother to drop the indiscreet Wyatt. By January 1992, when the photograph scandal was the talk of London, the affair with Wyatt was already over.

For Prince Andrew this seems to have been the last straw. On 19 March, 1992, two months after the Wyatt photos story, the Yorks announced that they had decided to separate. To a stunned public, this seemed to be a full acknowledgement of the duchess' adultery. Before this new information had had time to sink in, the public was hit with a bigger revelation.

DIANA DRIVEN TO FIVE SUICIDE BIDS BY 'UN-CARING CHARLES' shrieked the headline of the *Sunday Times* on 7 June 1992. The story beneath contained some of the most startling revelations from a new book by Andrew Morton, a royal journalist, entitled *Diana: Her True Story*. What made this book different from other similar works –

like Lady Colin Campbell's *Diana in Private* – was that it was plainly written with some co-operation from the Princess of Wales.

Morton had quite a story to tell. The book revealed that Diana had been doubtful about marrying Charles from the start. Since 1972, Charles had been friendly with Camilla Parker-Bowles; they were so close that they addressed one another as Fred and Gladys. Camilla was married to Andrew Parker-Bowles, a member of the queen's household, and Diana had known her since 1980. At first, Diana was unsuspicious, even when she learned that Camilla was reputed to 'vet' all Charles's girlfriends. She remained unsuspicious when Camilla asked her if she meant to hunt when she was at Highgrove (Prince Charles's new house), and looked relieved when Diana said no. But a few weeks before their wedding, she learned that Charles and Camilla were 'Fred and Gladys' to one another when Charles had sent her a get-well bouquet inscribed from Fred to Gladys. And when, on the eve of her wedding, she learned that Charles intended to give Camilla a bracelet inscribed G and F (which, according to an alternative source, stood for 'Girl Friday', another of Charles's pet nicknames for Camilla), it dawned on her with an awful sense of certainty that Camilla was her future husband's mistress, and that he had no intention of breaking off the relationship when he married. She came close to calling the wedding off the night before the ceremony.

When, on their honeymoon, photographs of Camilla fell out of Charles's diary, and when she noticed that he wore cufflinks with two 'Cs' intertwined – which he admitted had been given to him by a woman he had loved and lost – her worst suspicions were confirmed.

Understandably, she was shattered. Ever since her parents' divorce she had been afraid of love, but was willing to suspend her distrust and learn to become a caring wife and mother. Now it was obvious that she was simply the third in a triangle, and that, like so many women who had married princes of the British royal family, she was going to be expected to close her eyes to her husband's infidelities.

On the eve of the wedding, Charles allayed her fears when he sent her a signet ring and an affectionate note. But all the tension made her eat more than she intended to, then vomit it all up.

They spent the honeymoon on the royal yacht *Britannia*, and here again, she began to feel excluded. She wanted to spend time getting to know her husband – with whom she was by now deeply in love. Charles took along his fishing tackle and a pile of books by his mentor Laurens van der Post, who had written of the bushmen of South Africa, and had been a friend of the psychologist Carl Jung. They hardly ever seemed to be alone. Again, Diana's response to stress was to creep to the kitchen and eats bowl after bowl of ice cream.

What no one realised was that Diana was suffering from the nervous disorder called bulimia nervosa, which involves overeating, usually followed by vomiting. Its sufferers tend to experience extreme mood-swings, and may become suicidal.

Clearly, both Charles and Diana had problems. He had thought he was marrying an uncomplicated girl who would enjoy being Princess of Wales and then queen; to learn – as he soon did – that she had nervous problems must have been a shock. For her part, she thought she was marrying a kind of protective father figure who would help her to adjust to her new life. But he seemed to live on another plane, and although he took her for long walks and read her page after page by Jung and van der Post, she felt she was being talked down to.

But the major problem, of course, was her suspicion that her husband was still in love with Camilla Parker-Bowles, and meant to renew their relationship at the first opportunity. They began to have violent rows about Camilla. And once a newly married couple start having violents rows, the marriage has lost its chance of the kind of slow and idyllic growth that can form the basis of a lifelong partnership; the golden bowl has developed a crack.

What she now needed was some close support from her husband, a reassurance that all would be well. But Charles seemed unable to unwilling to offer such reassurance. He seemed to feel that she was suffering from a form of schoolgirl tantrums, and that what was really needed was that she should pull herself together. Most of the royal family seemed to feel much the same. On New Years Day, 1982, when she was three months pregnant with Prince William, she threatened suicide, and Charles accused her of being hysterical. When he went off riding on the Sandringham estate, she hurled herself down a long wooden staircase.

It was the Queen Mother, the major architect of the marriage, who found her lying dazed at the bottom and trembling with shock, and who summoned help. A hastily-summoned gynaecologist was able to assure everyone that both Diana and the foetus were unharmed.

Far from winning sympathy from her husband, it infuriated him as a piece of melodramatic hysteria. In a sense, the marriage ended then, less than a year after it had begun.

According to Lady Colin Campbell, in *Diana in Private*, Diana also felt that she was an outsider in the royal family. The Queen, says Lady Colin, had absolutely nothing in common with Diana, and 'the gulf between them grew worse and worse'. Princess Anne simply regarded Diana as 'an airhead and a lightweight' and could not understand why Charles had married her. But one day, when Diana dropped into the conversation at the dinner table a question about how they saw the role of the royal family in a united

Europe, they regarded her with puzzlement for a few moments, then went back to discussing hunting. Diana's increasing frustration is understandable.

Morton describes how Diana one day threw herself against a glass display cabinet, and how, during one argument with Prince Charles, she seized penknife and cut herself on the chest and thighs. Charles's reaction was to ignore her.

For Charles it must have seemed that the fairytale marriage had turned to a kind of hell. The sweet, shy twenty-year-old, who was supposed to adore him and be delighted that he had introduced her to a new and wonderful life turned out to be a vengeful neurotic who spent half her time in tears and was always complaining. He must have wished that he had taken his courage into his hands all those years before, and married Camilla, who thoroughly understood him.

The arrival of Prince William improved things for a while; Charles loved being a father, and was well suited to the role. Then there was a reaction, and Diana plunged back into depression. She began to see a psychiatrist (Jungian, naturally), but continued to lose weight. Diana and Charles moved between their two home, Kensington Palace and Highgrove, but they had so little social life that their butler described working for them as boring.

On the other hand, Charles continued to hunt with the Parker-Bowleses, and saw Camilla with a certain regularity. And Diana 'found a shoulder to lean and cry on' in her personal bodyguard, Sergeant Barry Manakee. Morton notes that 'the affectionate bond that built up between them did not go unnoticed either by Prince Charles or Manakee's colleagues'. Manakee was later transfered to other duties, and was killed in a motor cycle accident. No impropriety has ever been alleged, but it seemed clear that, lacking emotional support from her husband and the royal family, she felt a need to look for it elsewhere.

Camilla Parker-Bowles

The romance between Prince Andrew and Fergie provided a welcome diversion. Diana and Fergie became close friends, and Diana, now more confident, guided Fergie through the routine of being a 'royal'. In public, she was self-possessed and as charming as ever. But she still felt that she was a kind of royal cipher. There was the occasion when she prepared a surprise for the royal family when they were due to spend an evening watching ballet at Covent Garden, and she and leading dancer Wayne Sleep rehearsed a routine in secret at Kensington Palace. The audience gasped when Diana stepped out on to the stage in a silver silk dress, and danced a specially choreographed routine to a song 'Uptown Girl', revealing that she had the makings of a first-class ballerina. The audience applauded wildly, and she took eight curtain calls, even curtseying to the royal box. But Charles later told her he thought that it had all been undignified and 'showy'.

Even by 1987, it was becoming obvious to the press that the royal marriage was under some strain. Diana and Fergie came in for criticism for 'frivolity' when both were photographed at a race meeting poking a friend in the backside with their umbrellas. When Diana and a group of friends had a weekend party at the stately home of the parents of a young man named Philip Dunne, a gossip columnist reported that Diana had spent the weekend alone with him. When she was ambushed by a photographer as she emerged from a cinema with a group of friends that included a young man called David Waterhouse, Waterhouse leapt a pedestrian barrier and fled into the night, causing more gossip than if he had stayed put.

In 1987, her confidence fortified by a new doctor who seemed to be helping her to conquer her bulimia, Diana cornered Camilla Parker-Bowles at a birthday party and accused her of sleeping with her husband. Whether Camilla admitted it or not Morton does not record, but he tells us that the explosion helped Diana to come to terms with her jealousy and anger.

At about this time – in 1988 – a polo player named Captain James Hewitt came into Diana's life when he began to teach Princes William and Harry horsemanship. She visited his home in Devon, and they were soon the subject of suspicion on the part of the royal family. A colour sergeant later told the *News of the World* that he had been part of a surveillance team whose job was to spy on the couple and photograph them making love in the garden. Hewitt's friend Anna Pasternak later wrote a book – with his cooperation – in which she admitted that they had been lovers.

The reason for this oddly brash piece of behaviour seems to lie in Morton's comment that they drifted apart to the extent of marshalling rival battalions of friends in their support. On the same page, Morton comments that Prince Charles 'counts on' Andrew and Camilla Parker-Bowles for social support. Their home, Middlewich House, was only twelve miles from Highgrove House. A Sunday newspaper described the unmarked Ford estate car in which Charles frequently drove to Middlewich House.

When, in January 1992, Prince Andrew and Fergie visited the Queen at Sandringham to confess that their marriage was at and end – partly due to the latest press uproar about her relation with Steve Wyatt – the queen asked them for a two month 'cooling off' period before they announced their separation. This completed, the press was informed that this marriage was over. Yet still Charles and Diana were officially together, even though they lived apart.

When Morton's *Diana: Her True Story* was published, after serialisaton in the *Sunday Times*, it combined all these scandalous revelations with a glowingly positive assessment of the princess, in which her work for charity and her love for her children featured prominently. In this respect the book read like one of the countless glossy coffee table books that portrayed the royal family as practitioners of all the old fashioned virtues, but Morton, with the help of

Diana's friends, had taken this genre and cross-bred it with kiss-and-tell Hollywood scandal sheets. It sold massively, making Morton a wealthy man.

In the postscript to the paperback edition, Morton begins: 'The days of pretending were over forever.' The book, apparently, had led the couple to face up to the collapse of their marriage. From now on, they were to live separate lives.

That summer of 1992, Fergie was back in the news. 'Fergie's Stolen Kisses' shouted the *Daily Mirror* headline. An Italian long-lens paparazzo, Daniel Angeli, had snapped the Duchess with her financial adviser John Bryan, a tall prematurely balding Texan who had been a schoolfriend of Steve Wyatt. They were holidaying together, with the duchess' children, in a villa in the woods outside St Tropez. In one photo, Bryan kisses the duchess' toes. The duchess is topless in the shots. Fergie was already virtually unmentionable within the royal family, and the photographs made any reconciliation out of the question.

Then, just at the point when Fergie was squirming uncomfortably in the spotlight, it was switched back to Diana again. On 24 August, 1992, the *Sun* published an account of a taped conversation between Princess Diana and a second hand car dealer, James Gilbey.

'My Life Is Torture: Dianagate tape of love call reveals marriage misery' declared the headline. The conversation opens arrestingly:

GILBEY: And so, darling, what are the other's lows today?

DIANA: So that was it . . . I was very bad at lunch. And I nearly started blubbing. I just felt really sad and empty, and I thought: 'Bloody hell, after all I've done for this fucking family.'

On the 23 minute tape, Gilbey addresses her as 'Squidgey' (fourteen times) and 'Darling' (fifty-three times), and at one point they blow kisses to one another down the phone. He tells her that he hasn't played with himself for forty-eight hours, and that something was 'very strange and very lovely too'. Diana replies: 'I don't want to get pregnant.' 'Darling, that's not going to happen. All right? . . . You won't get pregnant.' After more general conversation, Gilbey tells her: 'Just have to wait till Tuesday.'

In fact, the tape had been recorded two years earlier, in December 1989, by an eavesdropper on the princess' mobile phone, using a device called a 'scanner'. It appeared to reveal that Diana had been on intimate terms with Gilbey while she and Charles were still living together. Yet the real interest of the tape lies in the enormous weariness Diana expresses regarding her in-laws: Here was further proof of the misery of the princess and the lack of communication at the heart of the monarchy. A debate about whether Diana and Gilbey did or did not have sex raged in the papers for weeks.

Oddly enough, the tape did Diana no harm with the British public. The suggestion that she had a lover added a dimension to her personality; the comment: 'I don't want to get pregnant' substituted the image of a woman capable of sexual passion for the demure schoolgirl persona that had made her seem a permanent virgin.

Prince Charles was reported to have been disgusted by the publicity, while Diana is on record as saying that it was a catharsis.

John Aubrey, in his *Brief Lives*, tells this anecdote about the court of Queen Elizabeth I:

'The Earle of Oxford, making low obeisance to Queen Elizabeth, happened to let a Fart, at which he was so ashamed that he went to Travell, 7 years. On his return the Queen welcomed him home, and sayd, "My Lord, I had forgot the Fart".'

On 9 December, 1992, Buckingham Palace announced 'with regret' that the Prince and Princes Wales had decided to separate.

Five weeks later, on Sunday 17 January, 1993, the *Sunday Mirror* and the *People* published in full a tape of another recorded telephone conversation, this time between Prince Charles and Camilla Parker-Bowles; like the Gilbey-Diana tape, it had been recorded by an eavesdropper. This conversation had, in fact, taken place on 17 December, 1989, two weeks before the Gilbey-Diana tape. It was considerably more explicit. When Camilla says: 'You're awfully good at feeling your way along', Charles replies: 'O, stop! I want to feel my way all along you, all over you, and up and down you and in and out . . . particularly in and out.' Camilla replies: 'O, that's just what I need at the moment.' Charles suggests: 'I'll just live inside your trousers or something. It would be much easier.' 'What, are you going to turn into a pair of knickers? You're going to come back as a pair of knickers.' 'Or', says Charles, 'God forbid, a Tampax. Just my luck! . . . to be chucked down a lavatory and go forever swirling around the top, never going down . . .'

In *Behind Palace Doors*, an even more revelatory book than Morton's, gossip columnist Nigel Dempster reports that when Charles heard about the tape, four days before it was published, he kept repeating: 'How can it all have gone wrong so quickly?' He may have been cheered when, after newspaper publication of the tape, a crowd of well-wishers at Sandringham shouted: 'Good old Charlie.' But a close friend commented: 'It was the worst moment of his life. He wanted to be taken seriously, to be given respect as a man. He sincerely believed that he had important things to say. He wanted to be thought profound. And in six minutes of private conversation, a conversation that was nobody's business but his and the woman to whom he was speaking, his reputation was ruined. Maybe it was a delusion that he

was something of a sage and a philosopher, but it was a
fairly harmless delusion. The downfall of a prince holds a
terrible fascination, but he really didn't deserve to be
destroyed so publicly.'

A passage from the *Encyclopedia Yearbook* for 1992
summarises succinctly the various problems encountered
by the royal family in 1992:

'During 1992 the media chronicled the breakdown of the
marriage of the Prince and Princess of Wales. A book
published in June – *Diana: Her True Story*, by a British
journalist, Andrew Morton, said that their marital problems
had provoked several suicide attempts by the princess.
Although Morton had not interviewed the princess, it
quickly became clear that he had spoken to several of
her closest friends, and that she had, tacitly at least,
authorized their disclosures. The stories about the couple,
amplified by aggressive reporting by tabloid newspapers,
added to the pressure on the royal family, which had seen
the divorce of the Princess Royal (the Prince of Wales's
sister) and the separation of the Duke and Duchess of York
earlier in 1992. Finally, on 9 December, Buckingham Palace
announced that the Prince and Princess of Wales would
separate. This announcement completed what the Queen
described as an "annus horribilis" in a rare public comment
of her troubles during a speech on the occasion of her 40th
anniversary on the throne. Not only had every one of the
first marriages of her children ended in separation, but she
also had to contend with a fire that destroyed much of the
interior of Windsor Castle on 20 November. The government agreed to finance the castle's restoration, in line with
established policy towards the royal castles, leaving the
queen to pay only for the furnishings that had been
destroyed within her private apartments. Controversy
over whether the Queen should make a greater contribu-
tion was only softened by an announcement six days later
that she had volunteered to give up her tax-free status. The

one undoubted source of joy to the royal family in the final weeks of a difficult year was the Princess Royal's wedding on 12 December to Commander Timothy Laurence, a former equerry (aide) to the Queen.'

The story is, of course, ongoing. The prince's 'downfall' was not as catastrophic as his friend seemed to suspect, and time has blurred the memory of the 'Camillagate' tape, although it was revived in 1995 by the divorce of Andrew and Camilla Parker-Bowles. And although a *Daily Mirror* poll indicated that 63 per cent of readers believed that Charles was not fit to be king, and that the crown should pass direct to Prince William, there seems to be little doubt that, when the time comes, Prince Charles will become King Charles III.

Princess Di continued to be as controversial as ever. After announcing that she was giving up public appearances and returning to private life, she continued to appear at many public events. And scandals continued to be associated with her name. Her friend Oliver Hoare complained to the police that a caller was ringing his home in the early hours of the morning, then hanging up without speaking; when the police investigated, they found that the calls were coming from Kensington Palace. And the year-old marriage of England's rugby captain Will Carling came to an end after reports that he was seeing a great deal of Diana.

The *Daily Mirror* poll also found that 42 per cent of readers thought that Britain would be no worse off without a royal family, and that one in six think the monarchy will not survive beyond the end of this century – another prophecy which – no doubt to the relief of the royal family – has so far showed no sign of coming true.